MULTINATIONAL ENTERPRISES AND INDUSTRIAL ORGANIZATION

MULTINATIONAL ENTERPRISES AND INDUSTRIAL ORGANIZATION

The Case of India

Nagesh Kumar

Sage Publications
New Delhi/Thousand Oaks/London

To my beloved mother, Shrilata

First published in 1994 by

Sage Publications India Pvt Ltd
M-32, Greater Kailash Market I
New Delhi 110048

Sage Publications Inc
2455 Teller Road
Thousand Oaks, California 91320

Sage Publications Ltd
6 Bonhill Street
London EC2A 4PU

Published by Tejeshwar Singh for Sage Publications India Pvt Ltd, lasertypeset by Print Line, Delhi and printed at Chaman Enterprises, Delhi.

Library of Congress Cataloging-in-Publication Data

Nagesh Kumar.
Multinational enterprises and industrial organization: the case of India/Nagesh Kumar.
p. cm.
Includes bibliographical references and index.
1. International business enterprises—Government policy—India. 2. Investments, Foreign—Government policy—India. I. Title.
HD2899.N339 338.8' 8854—dc20 1994 94-21364

ISBN: 81-7036-411-6 (India-hb)
0-8039-9183-5 (US-hb)

Contents

List of Abbreviations

ACP	African, Caribbean and Pacific
ASEAN	Association of South East Asian Nations
BOP	Balance of Payments
CCEA	Cabinet Committee on Economic Affairs
EC	European Community
EOU	Export Oriented Unit
EPZ	Export Processing Zone
ERP	Effective Rates of Protection
ESCAP	Economic and Social Commission for Asia and the Pacific
FB	Foreign Branch
FCEs	Foreign Controlled Enterprises
FCRC	Foreign Controlled Rupee Company
FDI	Foreign Direct Investment
FERA	Foreign Exchange Regulation Act
FIB	Foreign Investment Board
FIIS	Foreign Institutional Investors
FIPB	Foreign Investment Promotion Board
FOB	Free on Board
FS	Foreign Shares
FSU	Foreign Subsidiary
GCC	Gulf Cooperation Council
IMF	International Monetary Fund
LERMS	Liberalized Exchange Rate Mechanism
LCEs	Locally Controlled Enterprises
MES	Minimum Economic Scale
MIGA	Multilateral Investment Guarantee Agency
MNEs	Multinational Enterprises
NAFTA	North American Free Trade Area
NCAER	National Council of Applied Economic Research
NF	National Front
NIE	Newly Industrializing Economies
NIP	New Industrial Policy
OCB	Overseas Corporate Bodies

OGL	Open General License
OPIC	Overseas Private Investment Corporation (of the United States)
PUC	Paid-up Capital
RBI	Reserve Bank of India
SAARC	South Asian Association for Regional Cooperation
SAPTA	SAARC Preferential Trading Area
SCP	Market Structure-Conduct-Performance
TNC	Transnational Corporation
TDF	Technical Development Fund
UNCTC	United Nations Centre on Transnational Corporations
UN-TCMD	United Nations Transnational Corporations and Management Division (earlier UNCTC)

List of Tables

Preface to the Second Edition

This book is an updated version of a study first published under the title *Multinational Enterprises in India: Industrial Distribution, Characteristics, and Performance,* (London and New York: Routledge, 1990) which incorporated my doctoral dissertation completed at the Delhi School of Economics (DSE) in 1987. I have been prompted to bring out this edition because the foreign investment policy of the Indian government has changed considerably since the first publication of the book in April 1990. By publishing this edition in India, I hope to make it more widely available in the country than its western predecessor and to contribute to the current debate on the role of multinational enterprises in the context of the ongoing economic reforms. Besides updating the book in terms of the relevant policy changes, literature and data that have appeared since its first publication, a postscript has been added to comment on the new policies in the light of its empirical findings. Much of the analysis in the book has been made in the industrial organization framework. The title has been modified to highlight this fact.

I have accumulated a great deal of intellectual debt during the evolution of this work to the present form. My foremost gratitude is to Professor N.S. Siddharthan of the Institute of Economic Growth (IEG) and Professor Pulin Nayak of the Delhi School of Economics (DSE) who supervised my dissertation. I am also immensely indebted to Professor K.L. Krishna of DSE who introduced me to the subject and has been a constant source of inspiration and advice. I owe much to Professor John H. Dunning of the Universities of Reading and Rutgers, not only for his many valuable comments but also for the inspiration and encouragement to publish my doctoral dissertation. He was kind enough to commend this work in his foreword to the Routledge edition.

The work embodied in this study has been spread over my tenure at three institutions, namely, the Research and Information System (RIS) for Non-Aligned and Other Developing Countries, since August 1985; the National Institute of Science, Technology and Development Studies (NISTADS), 1984–85; and the Indian Institute of Public Administration (IIPA), 1981–84. The publication of this revised edition has been coordinated from the United Nations University—Institute for New Technologies (UNU/INTECH) in Maastricht where I am based since April 1993. My grateful thanks are due to the authorities and staff of these institutions for their understanding and generous support. The study has benefited immensely from the valuable comments and encouragement received from Dr V.R. Panchamukhi, Director, RIS at different stages. My stay at the erstwhile Corporate Studies Group of the IIPA, which has since become the Institute for Studies in Industrial Development (ISID), and interactions with Professor S.K. Goyal, its Director, have proved to be quite fruitful for the database of the study.

Different parts of this study have also benefited from the comments, suggestions, and reactions of Professors Alan Rugman (University of Toronto), K.K. Subrahmanian (Centre for Development Studies, Thiruvananthapuram), Ashok Desai (formerly in the Ministry of Finance), Homi Katrak (University of Surrey), Surendra Patel (formerly in the UNCTAD), B.N. Goldar (IEG), R.G. Nambiar (Sardar Patel Institute, Ahmedabad), Badal Mukherjee (DSE), Nirmal Chandra (Indian Institute of Management, Calcutta), Raj Sharma and V.L. Rao (RIS), and Rakesh Mohan (Ministry of Industry), among others.

A number of friends have contributed to the study in various ways. Among those who deserve special mention are K.S. Chalapati Rao (ISID), Brij Mohan Gupta (Central Board of Secondary Education), and Gurdip Singh (United News of India).

This edition would not have come out but for the keen personal interest of Mr Tejeshwar Singh, Managing Director, Sage Publications. I would also like to thank Ms Rosemary Nixon, Senior Editor, and Ms Gela Jacobson, Foreign Rights

Representative at Routledge, for providing the necessary permission.

Beena Pandey (RIS) has assisted me with careful reading of proofs and preparation of index, and Sachin Chaturvedi with updation of certain tables and references. Sanjay Sharma, Kiran Wagh, Sheela Malhotra, and E.V. Benny have provided secretarial support at different phases of the study.

Finally, I must express my gratitude to my parents for their encouragement. I would also like to thank Rachana, my wife, for supporting this venture as sincerely as my other undertakings which also remain unacknowledged.

Maastricht, The Netherlands
July 1994

Nagesh Kumar

Introduction

This study analyzes the industrial distribution, characteristics, and performance of affiliates of multinational enterprises (MNEs) in India. Multinational enterprises (foreign controlled enterprises) play an important role in economic activity in most developing countries. They account for 70 per cent of the manufacturing output in Zimbabwe, 63 per cent in Singapore, 44 per cent in Malaysia, 36 per cent in Venezuela, and 32 per cent in Brazil (UNCTC 1988). Even though India has received only a small proportion of the world foreign direct investment (FDI) stock, MNE affiliates constitute an important and prosperous segment of the corporate sector. They dominate in certain branches of manufacturing, such as medicines and pharmaceuticals, dry batteries, toilet preparations, several types of machinery and equipment, automobile tyres and tubes, and plastic raw materials.

MNEs are characterized by gigantic scale of operations, large research budgets, and geographical as well as product diversity. They own intangible assets, such as established brand names, proprietary technology, a reservoir of skills, and an 'organization capable of mastering complex tasks', which gives them an edge over their rivals (Vernon 1977: ch. 2). MNEs are equipped with international information networks and respond to global opportunities with centralized decision-making. Their headquarters are usually located in the industrialized market economies.

These characteristics of MNEs have implications for the industrial distribution, conduct, and performance of their affiliates in host countries. MNEs are likely to be concentrated in industries in which their intangible assets provide them with an edge over their local counterparts (subject to the presence of locational and internalization incentives) (see Hymer 1960 published in 1976; Caves·1971, 1974a; Dunning 1979; Rugman 1981). Because of their intangible assets, their competitive rivalry and other aspects of conduct are different from those of their local counterparts. The recent literature, therefore, has posited foreign ownership as an element of market structure influencing other aspects of structure, conduct, and performance (Caves *et al.* 1980; Newfarmer and Marsh 1981). Further, if the competitive rivalry and conduct of MNE affiliates and local firms are dissimilar they may constitute different 'strategic groups' (Caves and Porter 1977) in an industry and enjoy differential protection from entry barriers. Hence, their performance could also differ.

It is in this broad framework that the present study analyzes the industrial distribution, distinguishing characteristics, and relative performance of MNEs in Indian manufacturing. More specifically, it examines to what extent the postulates of the theory of international operations of the firm, particularly the recent advancements within the framework of the internalization paradigm and government policy factors, are able to explain the inter-industry pattern of MNE presence in Indian manufacturing industries. Using appropriate univariate and multivariate statistical techniques, this study examines the conduct of MNE affiliates (or foreign enterprises) relative to that of local firms in terms of the scale of operation, advertising, in-house R&D, financing, retention, choice of technique, and employee compensation; and relative performance in terms of profitability, growth, export, and linkage creation. The determinants of profit margins of MNE affiliates and local firms are analyzed, and explanations sought for the superior performance of the former. The study explores whether differential protection enjoyed by the two groups of firms from entry barriers explains the profitability differences. Finally, it examines the export behaviour of the two groups of firms in order to assess their role in promoting India's exports.

The Analytical Framework

The analyses of the factors that explain the inter-industry distribution of intensity of FDI (from the home country and in the host country) have drawn from the theory of international operations of the firm. This theory makes international operations conditional to ownership of certain intangible assets which gives the owning firm an advantage over local firms (Hymer 1960 published in 1976; Kindleberger 1969; Caves 1971, 1974a). The revenue productivity of these advantages is appropriated through exports in the initial stages of the product cycle and through foreign production when locational factors make it more profitable (Vernon 1966). Foreign production can be accomplished through renting out (licensing) the intangible asset to unassociated local firms or through FDI, that is, setting up an affiliate (which may take the form of an overseas branch, subsidiary, or a joint venture) and, thus, internalizing the transfer of the intangible asset. The choice between the two modes is mainly determined by the relative transaction cost involved in the market transfer (Buckley and Casson 1976; Dunning 1979; Williamson 1981; Rugman 1981). The higher the transaction cost, the greater the incentive to internalize (or resort to FDI). Therefore, FDI is expected to be prominent in those industries in which intangible assets with high internalization and locational incentives are important. The licensing mode of foreign operations is similarly expected to be preferred in branches where intangible assets with high locational incentives (but with low internalization incentives) are present. A rigorous test of these predictions, however, has not yet been possible mainly due to the difficulty in classifying intangible assets between those with high or low internalization incentives.

The ownership of intangible assets, thus, enjoys a central place in explaining the process of internationalization of firms in the theory. The ownership advantages of MNEs not only explain their very existence in countries other than their homes, but may also have certain implications for the behaviour of their foreign affiliates compared to their local counterparts. For instance, the asset bundles of MNE affiliates differ from those of their local rivals because of their ownership of intangible assets, such as access to the goodwill associated with brand names, technology, and the reservoir of organizational skills of the parent firm. In order to maximize the revenue productivity of their asset bundles, MNE affiliates may adopt a non-price mode of rivalry based on product differentiation (Caves 1974b). Their pricing is, thus, likely to be monopolistic and could include a monopoly rent on account of the ownership of intangible assets. Their profit margins, therefore, are expected to be higher. The access of MNEs to international capital markets may result in different leverage ratios of their affiliates, depending upon the relative cost of funds in the host country. Their access to information on world markets, and to international marketing networks, makes it possible for them to exploit the international division of labour more fruitfully. Hence, the degree of export orientation and raw material sourcing of their operations could be different. Their advanced organizational skills can lead to different inventory and liquidity ratios.

In addition to the ownership of intangible assets there are other reasons which lead one to expect differences in the behaviour of MNE affiliates and their local counterparts. For instance, depending upon the degree of centralization of an MNE's organization, the parent firm may retain the power to take certain strategic decisions, such as the choice of technology, investment priorities, R&D, raw material sourcing, exports, and profit repatriation (Newfarmer and Marsh 1981). These decisions are likely to be based on international financial and market considerations, relative tax rates, and the global strategy of the MNE which aims at maximizing global profits. Gorecki (1976, 1980) found that entry and diversification decisions of MNE affiliates in Canada could be explained less satisfactorily in terms of local conditions, than in the case of their local counterparts. Howe and McFetridge (1976) reported similar results pertaining to MNE decisions to undertake R&D in Canada. Furthermore, their grooming in an environment of capital abundance and labour scarcity may be reflected in their choice of technology and on the factor proportions employed by them. Levels of employee compensation may also be higher for the same reason.

Thus, the behavioural characteristics of MNE affiliates are likely to be quite different from those of their local counterparts engaged in similar activities. Hence, the two could constitute different 'strategic groups' in an industry of the type proposed by Caves and Porter (1977), Newman (1978), and Porter (1979). Caves *et al.* (1980), and Newfarmer and Marsh (1981), therefore, have considered foreign ownership to be an element of market structure, like concentration, product differentiation and entry barriers, affecting other aspects of market structure, conduct, and performance. However, a simultaneity problem may exist in the relationship between foreign ownership and other aspects of market structure, because the incidence of FDI itself is dependent upon structural factors. MNEs enjoy an edge over their local rivals in overcoming entry barriers because they possess certain intangible assets. Therefore, they are concentrated in industries with high entry barriers, such as advertising, technology, skill, and capital intensity (Caves 1982). Caves *et al.* (1980), Saunders (1982), and Gupta (1983) have taken note of the possible simultaneity problem by specifying foreign ownership as an endogenous variable in larger industrial organization models of Canada.

In this study a slightly different approach is used to overcome the simultaneity problem. First, the determinants of inter-industry differences in foreign shares in terms of intangible assets and locational advantages using the postulates of internalization theory are analysed. Next, the differences between MNE affiliates and their local counterparts are examined in terms of a large number of structural and behavioural characteristics in the comparative static framework. The simultaneity problem can arise only in cases where behaviour of MNE affiliates is significantly different from their local counterparts. Therefore, only the variables and aspects that distinguish MNE affiliates and local firms are specified as endogenous and are subjected to further analysis.

Multinational Enterprises: A Definition

This study deals with those affiliates of MNEs in India in which they have a controlling interest, or in which their investment is classified as FDI (as opposed to portfolio or non-equity forms of foreign investment). MNEs have two types of controlled affiliates abroad: first, foreign branches, that is, undertakings not registered under the local laws; and second, affiliates registered in the host country which may be wholly or partly owned by the MNE. In the latter case, however, the proportion of equity participation should be large enough to ensure control and to qualify as FDI. Different countries have varying cut-off points for the minimum proportion of equity holding to distinguish FDI from portfolio investment. These range between 10 per cent and 50 per cent. These percentages are essentially rules of thumb because in reality the degree of control depends upon factors such as the pattern of distribution of local shares, the nature of agreements, and the degree of technological dependence. Hence, the minimum proportion of equity necessary for securing control may vary from case to case.

In India, the Reserve Bank of India (RBI), defines two types of foreign controlled enterprises (FCEs) or controlled affiliates of MNEs: (*a*) foreign branches (FBs), as companies which are incorporated outside the country but have a place of business in India; and (*b*) foreign controlled rupee companies, as joint stock companies registered in India in which 25 per cent or more of equity capital is held abroad by a foreign company or its nominee or 40 per cent is held outside India. The former category of FCEs, that is, FBs, has steadily lost its importance as a result of the enforcement of the Foreign Exchange Regulation Act (1973) which required FBs to convert themselves into rupee companies. Now, FBs are permitted to operate only in service sectors, such as banking, transport and communications, and their role in the industrial sector is negligible. As the present work is confined to the industrial sector, foreign controlled enterprise (FCE) refers only to a company registered in India with at least 25 per cent equity held with the parent MNE. *The terms FCE and MNE affiliates will be used interchangeably*. The definition of FCE adopted here (i.e., a minimum 25 per cent held by the parent MNE) is consistent with that used by numerous studies for different countries such as, Newfarmer and Mueller (1975), Cohen (1975), Lall (1976), Connor (1977), Lall and Streeten (1977), Newfarmer and Marsh (1981), Chen (1983), Stopford and Dunning (1983), and Fairchild and Sosin (1986).

The Database

For a rigorous treatment of the objectives of the study and verification of the theoretical propositions outlined, data on foreign shares and structural characteristics of industry is required. Data on the comparative performance of FCEs and local firms in terms of a large number of parameters for a cross-section of manufacturing industries is also needed. The official Indian database of FCEs, however, does not satisfy these needs (see Appendix I). To overcome this problem two variable sets were created on the industry and group characteristics of 54 manufacturing industries on the basis of unpublished firm-level financial statistics of 1,334 medium and large non-government public limited companies (in the manufacturing sector) for the period 1975–76 to 1980–81 made available by the RBI. The coverage extended to all non-government, non-financial public limited companies with paid-up capital of Rs 10 million and above, and a sample from the smaller companies. In all, the companies included in the survey accounted for 86 per cent of the paid-up capital of all public limited companies in the Indian private sector in 1979–80. Appendix I provides details of the industry classification, identification of FCEs, methodology of computation, and measurements of variables included in the two sets of data.

An Overview

The subject matter of the study has been organized in seven chapters. The host country policy often plays an important role in shaping the magnitude, pattern, and even impact of operations of foreign enterprises. Chapter 1 reviews the evolution of the Indian government's policy towards foreign collaborations in the post-Independence period. The chapter also examines the influence of government policy on trends and patterns of FDI in the economy.

Chapter 2 deals with the economic significance of FCEs in the Indian manufacturing sector. Existing estimates of the share of FCEs in Indian industry are reviewed and more recent estimates are provided of their shares in assets, sales, and profits. The share of FCEs in the sales of 54 manufacturing industries (at the three-digit level) are also computed.

Chapter 3 analyzes the determinants of inter-industry distribution of foreign shares. The theory of international operations the firm is outlined (particularly the recent internalization approach), and its relevance is examined in the present context. Testable hypotheses are formulated in the light of the postulates of this theory. The new theory expects FDI to be concentrated in industries where the intangible assets of firms provide them with a competitive edge, and where internalization and locational incentives are present. In the absence of internalization incentives foreign expansion is accomplished through the licensing of intangible assets. Therefore, an attempt is made to classify the broad categories of intangible assets into those with high or low internalization incentives on the basis of possible transaction costs involved. For a more complete test of the predictions, this study also specifies licensing as a dependent variable. Findings of the statistical analysis are presented for both the dependent variables, FDI and licensing.

Chapter 4 analyzes the distinctive characteristics of FCEs. It discusses the reasons for expecting differences between FCEs and their local counterparts in terms of different aspects of conduct and performance. Hypotheses are formulated concerning the nature of the differences between FCEs and local firms in terms of 15 parameters representing diverse characteristics, such as scale of operation, advertising, R&D intensity, profit margins, growth rates, choice of technique, employee compensation, vertical local inter-firm linkages and import dependence, export performance, leverage and retention ratios, tax planning, inventory, and liquidity management. The empirical analysis is conducted in two stages. In the first stage the significance of mean difference for each of the 15 parameters is evaluated in a univariate context. However, findings of univariate tests may be misleading on account of interaction of some of these variables. The possible interaction among variables is controlled in a multivariate framework in the second stage.

Chapter 5 analyzes the determinants of profit margins of FCEs and local firms to seek explanations for the higher profit margins of the former. Profit margins of FCEs may be higher because of their superior ability accruing from the possession of rent-yielding assets. Another possibility is that FCEs and local firms pursue different competitive strategies and entry barriers protect them differently. To examine which of these possibilities actually explains the systematic profitability differences, the profit margins of the two groups of firms are regressed on different sources of entry barriers identified in the literature. The statistical significance of the differences in the intercept and slope coefficients of profit functions of FCEs and local firms is examined through covariance analysis.

Chapter 6 analyzes the determinants of export behaviour of FCEs and local firms to find out whether FCEs help the country to export products which would not have been exported in their absence. The hypotheses to explain inter-industry variation in export performance of FCEs and local firms are formulated in terms of industry and firm characteristics in the framework of neo-classical and neo-technology theories of international trade.

Chapter 7 summarizes the major findings of the study and their implications for further research, and indicates their policy applications. It also suggests some directions for further work on the subject.

Finally, the postscript comments upon the new foreign investment policy in the light of the empirical findings of this work and other recent studies. In view of the current foreign exchange crisis, a more focused approach to attract export-oriented FDI is recommended. Various issues and factors involved in attracting such investment and relevant policy measures are also discussed.

1

Government Policy and Foreign Direct Investment in India

Host government policy plays an important role in influencing the magnitude, importance, pattern, form, and impact of FDI on the economy. In accordance with the country's developmental objectives the Government of India has pursued a selective policy towards foreign enterprises since Independence. This chapter provides a brief overview of the evolution of government policy towards FDI, and its impact on the trends and patterns of FDI. This discussion is meant to serve as a background for the later analysis.

Evolution of Government Policy: 1948–1994

The Indian government's attitude towards foreign investment has been changing in the post-Independence period and three distinct phases are discernible: the period from Independence up to the late 1960s, which was marked by gradual liberalization; the period from the late 1960s to the 1970s, which was characterized by a more selective stance; and the 1980s, which once again heralded a liberal policy. In the 1990s the policy has been liberalized further and made more open and transparent.

The Phase of Liberalization: 1948–1967

The Industrial Policy Resolution (April 1948) recognized the role of foreign capital in aiding rapid industrialization of the country. However, a need for regulation was felt and a legislation to regulate foreign capital in 'national interest' was proposed. The legislation was meant to ensure that majority ownership and effective control remained, *as a rule*, in Indian hands. In the Foreign Investment Policy Statement (April 1949), however, the government showed no intention of adopting any legislation for the regulation of foreign capital. This, perhaps, was an outcome of the economic crisis resulting from the partition of the country and the shyness of local enterprise.[1] Instead, foreign investment was considered *necessary* (earlier, merely important) for supplementing Indian capital and securing 'scientific, technical and industrial knowledge and capital equipment'. Foreign investment was, thus, encouraged on mutually advantageous terms. Though majority ownership in local hands was still preferred, it was no more the *rule*. Foreign investors were assured of unrestricted remittances of profits and dividends, fair compensation in case of acquisition, and were promised 'national treatment'. The non-discriminatory treatment accorded to foreign capital was, however, strongly resented by domestic capital. Local enterprises found it difficult to compete with their foreign rivals in the consumer goods industries, such as soaps (Lever Brothers) and fountain pen inks (Parker Pen Co.), and wanted the entry of foreign enterprises restricted to areas where they did not have the capability.[2]

The new Industrial Policy Resolution (April 1956) was drawn up in accordance with the goal of a 'socialistic pattern' of society adopted by the Parliament in 1954. The resolution earmarked a number of important industries for the public sector, thus, reducing the scope of operation of the private—local as well as foreign—sector. However, the Resolution did not make any further distinction within the private sector, or between domestic and foreign enterprises.

The foreign exchange crisis of 1957–58 led to a further liberalization in the government's attitude towards foreign capital. In a bid to attract foreign investment to finance the foreign exchange component of projects, a host of incentives and concessions were given. For instance, the Indo-US Convertability Agreement was signed in 1957. In the same year a number of tax concessions were made to foreign firms which affected salaries, wealth tax, and super tax. Corporate taxes on income and royalties were reduced in the 1959 and 1961 budgets. Double taxation avoidance agreements to lower the tax burden of foreign investors were signed with most of the source countries, namely, the United States, Sweden, Denmark, the erstwhile West Germany, and Japan. India received a number of Western industrial and trade missions and sent an industrial mission abroad in order to attract foreign capital to the country. The Indian Investment Centre, with offices in major investor countries, was set up in 1961 to promote foreign investment in India.

Anticipating the continuation of the foreign exchange bottleneck and its effect on the Third Five Year Plan projects, the government issued a list of industries in 1961 (taking into account the gaps in capacity in relation to plan targets) in which foreign investment was to be welcomed. These included some of the more profitable industries earlier reserved for the public sector, such as drugs, aluminium, heavy electrical equipment, fertilizers, and synthetic rubber. An Officer on Special Duty was deputed in the Ministry of Commerce and Industry to provide prompt and reliable guidance to foreign investors on investment opportunities. It was clearly stated that foreign investment to cover the foreign exchange cost of plant and machinery in approved projects would be welcome. The proportion of foreign held equity was to depend upon the sophistication of technology and the requirement of foreign exchange. Local majority ownership, though *welcome* was not to be insisted upon.[3] In fact, proposals involving foreign financial collaborations enjoyed a premium in government approvals during those years (Kidron 1965: 262; IIPA 1983, ch. 4).

This was the period when Western MNEs started showing interest in India. In the early 1950s their response was lukewarm except in the case of a one-shot investment in oil refineries (Kidron 1965: 102, 157). In the period after 1957, however, substantial foreign investment started flowing in, even into non-essential items. During the period 1957 to 1963,

45 per cent of consents for new capital issues involved foreign investments, while the proportion for the period from 1951 to 1963 was 34 per cent (Kidron 1965: 258). The Hathi Committee (1975) noted that it was in this period that most foreign drug firms set up manufacturing subsidiaries in the country.

The Restrictive Phase: 1968–1979

Liberalization of the policy towards foreign capital continued till the mid-1960s. As a result, the outflow on account of remittances of dividends, profits, royalties, and technical fees grew sharply and became a significant proportion of the foreign exchange account of the country. These remittances caught the government's attention in the course of another foreign exchange crisis in the late 1960s. This led to the streamlining of procedures for foreign collaboration approvals and the adoption of a more restrictive attitude.

On the recommendation of the Mudaliar Committee on Foreign Collaborations (1966), a new agency called the Foreign Investment Board (FIB) was set up in 1968 to deal with all cases involving foreign investment or collaboration except those in which total investment in share capital exceeded Rs 20 million and where the proportion of foreign equity exceeded 40 per cent. These cases were to be referred to the Cabinet Committee. A sub-committee of the FIB was empowered to approve cases of foreign collaboration in which the proportion of foreign held equity did not exceed 25 per cent and where total equity investment was up to Rs 10 million. The administrative ministries were authorized to approve cases involving purely technical collaboration. Foreign investments unaccompanied by technology were not to be favoured.

Three illustrative lists which demarcated industries were issued: (*a*) where no foreign collaboration was considered necessary, (*b*) where only technical collaboration could be permitted, and (*c*) where foreign investment might be permitted.[4] In the latter two cases a permissible range of royalty payments was also specified for different items which generally did not exceed 5 per cent. The permitted duration of the collaborations was reduced from 10 to 5 years and their renewals were restricted. Restrictive clauses concerning the sub-licensing of technology in the country, and exports (except to those countries where the technology supplier already had affiliates) were not to be permitted (Government of India, Ministry of Industry 1982).

In 1976, a Technical Evaluation Committee was set up to assist the FIB in screening foreign collaboration proposals; the committee included representation from various scientific agencies such as the Council of Scientific and Industrial Research, and the Department of Science and Technology. The exclusive use of Indian consultancy, wherever available, was also recommended. If in addition foreign consultants were required, the Indian consultants were still to be retained as prime consultants. A new Patent Act was enacted in 1970 which abolished 'product' patents in foods, chemicals, and drugs, and reduced the life of process patents from 16 to 7 years. (14 years in other cases).[5] It contained provisions for a worldwide search of patent literature to establish the novelty of a product or process, and compulsory licensing after three years.

One implication of the delegation of the power of approval of foreign collaborations involving up to 40 per cent foreign equity to the committee of officials, namely, the FIB, was that proposals with more than 40 per cent foreign equity were considered to be special cases and hence, were to be referred to the Cabinet Committee. This ruling encouraged the restriction of foreign participation to 40 per cent, and marked the beginning of the phase of restricting foreign equity to this level. From February 1972 the government began approving the expansion plans of those companies with majority foreign equity, subject to their accepting a dilution of foreign equity by raising a certain proportion of the estimated cost of expansion through issue of additional equity to Indian nationals.[6] The government's decisions regarding industrial policy in 1970, which were made more concrete in 1973,[7] sought to further restrict the activities of foreign companies (along with those of large local industrial houses) to a select group of core (or Appendix I) industries. These industries were considered to be of 'basic, critical and strategic importance'. In the same year the Foreign Exchange Regulation Act (1973), FERA, was enacted which influenced the operations of foreign firms more than any other policy instrument. It became the corner-stone of the regulatory framework for foreign investment in later years. In view of the profound implications of FERA on the organization of the foreign controlled sector it is discussed at length.

The Foreign Exchange Regulation Act (1973)

According to its preamble FERA was 'an Act to consolidate and amend the law regulating certain payments, dealing in foreign exchange and securities, transactions indirectly affecting foreign exchange and the import and export of currency and bullion, for the conservation of the foreign exchange resources of the country and the proper utilization thereof in the interest of the economic development of the country.' Section 29 of FERA covered all existing non-banking branches (FBs),[8] and companies incorporated under the Indian Companies Act with more than 40 per cent foreign equity participation. All such companies that existed when FERA came into force (on 1 January 1974) were required to obtain RBI permission to continue their business. The permission was subject to the Indianization or dilution of their foreign equity as per government guidelines for implementation of the Act issued in 1973 and amended in 1976. These guidelines required FBs to transfer all their businesses to Indian companies that had upto 40 per cent foreign equity. Rupee (Indian) companies were also directed to dilute their foreign equity to a maximum of 40 per cent. Companies operating in the core sector (Appendix I industries), tea plantations, and those engaged in manufacturing activities based on sophisticated technology or predominantly producing for exports were, however, permitted to retain up to 51 or 74 per cent foreign equity. FERA, therefore, put a general ceiling of 40 per cent on foreign equity participation in the country. The Act allowed only a limited number of companies engaged in specified activities to have more than 40 per cent foreign equity. Only these companies were to be given differential treatment under the industrial licensing policy.[9] All other companies incorporated in India with foreign equity upto 40 per cent would be free to expand, diversify, and operate in any field like any local company. An assurance to this effect was made in the Industrial Policy Statement of 1977.

The process of Indianization of FBs operating in the country and the dilution of foreign equity in other rupee companies which FERA sparked off, brought about a drastic change in the organizational structure of the foreign controlled sector in India. One significant outcome was that all companies operating in the country (except foreign airline, shipping and banking companies) were incorporated under the Indian Companies Act. This put a stop to the alleged tax free repatriation of profits in the form of 'head-office expenses' by FBs. This provision vitally affected the tea plantation industry which was dominated by 114 British tea companies (FBs). Since the reorganization, the business of these FBs has been taken over by 45 companies incorporated in India with up to 74 per cent foreign equity.[10] A number of MNEs that were maintaining branch offices in India—to monitor investment opportunities and oversee their investments in other companies but without any manufacturing activity—had to wind-up. Therefore, the branch as a form of operation by foreign companies became virtually extinct except in the service sectors.

Another aspect of the enforcement of FERA was that of the 881 companies which sought RBI permission to continue their business only about 150 (including tea companies) were permitted to retain higher levels of foreign equity.[11] Only these companies remained within the ambit of FERA. Others diluted their foreign equity to 40 per cent as per RBI directives. These companies were now able to operate, expand, and diversify in any industry open to other local private firms. Thus, for most foreign companies FERA provided an opportunity to become 'Indian' and to expand. Hence, most of them readily agreed to dilute the foreign equity to 40 per cent.[12] That did not mean, however, that they ceased to be foreign controlled. First, the criterion of 40 per cent share holding was arbitrary. Effective control over a joint stock company can, sometimes, be exercised with as little as 10 per cent block share holding. Both the Monopolies and Restrictive Trade Practices Act (MRTP) and the RBI consider 25 per cent equity holding to be adequate for exercising effective control. Second, FERA dilutions in most cases were effected not by the sale of foreign held shares to Indian nationals but through the issue of fresh shares. This process of share allotment ensured that the new share holdings were as widely dispersed as possible. In addition, the clauses inserted in the Articles of Association just before the dilution of shares gave special rights to the foreign share holders. Therefore, the dilution of foreign share holdings did not necessarily imply a reduction in foreign management control (See Chadhuri (1979); Goyal (1979); Kumar (1982)).

The Opening Up of the 1980s

Almost throughout the 1970s the government's attention was focused on the enforcement of FERA. Towards the end of the decade, however, India's failure to significantly step-up the volume and proportion of manufactured exports in the context of the second oil price shock began to worry policy-makers. It led to the realization that the international competitiveness of Indian goods was poor because of growing technological obsolescence and inferior product quality, limited range, and high cost. These were in part due to the highly protected local market.[13] Another limiting factor lay in the fact that marketing channels in industrialized countries were dominated by MNEs.[14] The government intended to deal with the situation by: (*a*) emphasizing the modernization of plant and equipment through liberalized imports of capital goods and technology, (*b*) exposing Indian industry to competition by gradually reducing import restrictions and tariffs and (*c*) assigning a greater role to MNEs in the promotion of manufactured exports by encouraging them to set up export-oriented units. This strategy was reflected in policy pronouncements made in the 1980s.

The Industrial Policy Statements of 1980 and 1982, for instance, announced a liberalization of licensing rules, a host of incentives, and exemption from foreign equity restrictions under FERA to 100 per cent export-oriented units. A major amendment of the MRTP Act in 1984 severely curtailed its scope. Some 25 industries were delicensed in 1985. It was decided that four more export processing zones (EPZ) should be set up in addition to the two existing ones, at Kandla (set up in 1965) and Santacruz (set up in 1972), to attract MNEs to start export-oriented units. The import-export policies of these years greatly liberalized the import of raw materials and capital goods by gradually expanding the list of items on the Open General License (OGL). In 1984 nearly 150 items and in 1985, 200 capital goods were added to the OGL list. Tariffs on imports of various capital goods were also slashed in 1985.[15] Restrictions on imports of designs and drawings were removed.

Parallel to the liberalization of trade policies there was an increasingly receptive attitude towards foreign investments and collaborations.[16] Policy guidelines were issued in November 1980, and thereafter, to streamline foreign collaboration approvals. The power to approve foreign collaborations not involving an outflow of more than Rs 5 million in foreign exchange and without any foreign equity participation was delegated to the administrative ministries.[17] In January 1987 this figure was further raised to Rs 10 million. Rules concerning payment of royalties and lumpsum technical fees were also relaxed.[18] Tax rates on royalties were reduced from 40 per cent to 30 per cent in the 1986 budget. A degree of flexibility was introduced in the policy concerning foreign equity participation, and exceptions to the general ceiling of 40 per cent on foreign equity were allowed on the merit of individual investment proposals.[19] To facilitate the flow of superior technology to existing industry the Cabinet Committee on Economic Affairs (CCEA) decided in December 1986 to permit foreign equity participation even in existing Indian companies employing superior technology. The equity participation under the new policy was, however, to be subject to certain conditions intended to make sure that this objective was fulfilled.[20] The employment of foreign nationals was also made much easier.[21]

A number of steps were taken to remove procedural bottlenecks in 1989. Customs tariffs on general projects, and machinery and components were reduced by 10 per cent ad valorem and concessions in tariffs in the electronic sector were extended to 35 more types of equipment in the February 1989 budget. The cement and aluminium industries were decontrolled and broadbanding in respect of industrial licensing was extended to production of white goods. The Technical Development Fund (TDF) Scheme was liberalized in April 1988 and March 1989 to allow for import of technology and capital goods upto the foreign exchange equivalent of Rs 30 million with a provision for further relaxation in deserving cases.[22]

Approvals for opening liaison offices by foreign companies in India were liberalized and procedures for outward remittances of royalties, technical fees, and dividends were streamlined. New procedures were introduced enabling direct application by a foreign investor even before choosing an Indian partner. The Finance Minister addressed a seminar on investment opportunities in India for US companies in New York in April 1989.

In order to expedite the flow of Japanese private investment and technology, the government announced the setting up of a 'fast channel' in May 1988 for their speedy clearance. The government also announced measures to streamline the remittance process and exempted export profits from income tax in order to attract Japanese corporations to produce in India for export, in the context of the strong yen.[23] The fast channel mechanism was subsequently also extended to other major home countries of foreign investors: first to erstwhile West Germany and later to USA, UK and France.[24]

As a result of these measures the investment climate in the country gradually improved. An OPIC (Overseas Private Investment Corporation of the United States) mission visited India during February-March 1983 with representations from major US MNEs active in oil exploration, food processing, computers, solar and wind energy generation, pharmaceuticals, coal mining, gear manufacture, diamond cutting, machine tools, etc.[25] In April 1985 the European Management Foundation organized a round table on India in New Delhi which was attended by 140 top MNE executives. Subsequently, a number of international business delegations visited India to explore investment opportunities. As a result of the streamlining of procedures and liberalization of attitude the rejection rate in foreign collaboration approvals came down from 30 per cent to between 5 and 8 per cent.[26]

Structural Adjustment and Globalization: 1990s

In December 1989 the National Front (NF) headed by Mr V.P. Singh came into power. The new government intended to carry forward the process of liberalization and streamline procedures relating to foreign investments. The Industry Minister in his speeches at a round table on India at the World Economic Forum in Davos in February 1990 and at the UNCTC round table in New Delhi in March 1990, and the Prime Minister in his address to the World Economic Forum at its national meeting on India in New Delhi in April 1990 indicated the government's plan to grant automatic approval to FDI proposals involving up to 40 per cent foreign equity.[27] In the New Import-Export Policy (1990–93) issued on 30 March 1990, eighty-two more capital goods were brought under OGL taking the total to 1,343 items. Under the TDF scheme the limit for import of designs and drawings was raised from Rs 3 million to Rs 10 million with an overall ceiling of Rs 30 million.[28]

New industrial policy measures for the debureaucratization and greater transparency of foreign investment approvals were announced in Parliament on 31 May 1990. These measures included abolition of industrial licensing for new units for fixed investment of up to Rs 250 million (Rs 750 million for export-oriented units (EOUs) and units located in recognized backward areas). An import entitlement of up to 30 per cent of the total value of plant and machinery, and for import of raw materials and spare parts to the extent of 30 per cent of the value of production (in addition to consumption of OGL items) was to be permitted. No clearance would be needed for concluding a foreign collaboration (licensing) agreement provided the royalty payment was restricted to 5 per cent on domestic sales and 8 per cent on exports. For proposals involving lumpsum payments, the required government clearance would be communicated within a month. Foreign equity investment up to 40 per cent was to be allowed on an automatic basis provided the landed value of imported capital goods did not exceed 30 per cent of the value of plant and machinery.[29] The government also proposed to issue a positive list of industries where foreign investment would be welcome.

These measures however, could not be implemented. The government was faced with a crisis and ultimately fell in November 1990 when a minority government headed by Mr Chandra Sekhar came to power. This government decided not to implement the proposal of automatic permission for foreign investment up to 40 per cent.[30] The minority government lasted only till March 1991 but was requested to continue as caretaker till a new government assumed office.

In the second half of the financial year 1990–91, India entered a period of severe balance of payments crisis. A rapid increase in external debt coupled with political uncertainty led international credit rating agencies to lower India's rating both for short- and long-term borrowings. Moody's down graded India in October 1990, from Prime–1 to Prime–2 (medium risk). In March, India's rating was further lowered from Prime–2 to Prime–3 for short-term borrowings and from BAA1 to BAA3 for long-term debt. In May 1991, Standard & Poor lowered India's rating on long-term senior public debt to a double bi plus (BBI +) from a triple bi minus (BBBI –), and short-term senior public debt to a single bi from a credit rating of a -3i.[31] The erosion of international confidence in the Indian economy not only made borrowings in international commercial markets difficult but also adversely affected the inflow of funds from non-resident Indians (NRIs). In the financial year 1990–91, NRI deposits registered an accretion of only about US$ 229 million compared to $1.3 billion in 1989–90. Net outflow of NRI deposits started in October 1990 and continued throughout 1991. In the period April to June 1991 alone there was a net outflow of nearly one billion dollars from NRI accounts.[32] The Gulf War which broke out in January 1991 exacerbated the balance of payments crisis by leading to a rise in petroleum prices, and a virtual stoppage of remittances from Indian workers in the Gulf.

These developments especially the sudden flight of NRI deposits depleted India's foreign exchange reserves and brought the country to the verge of default with respect to external payments liability. The default was averted by resorting to borrowings from the IMF (International Monetary Fund) under the standby arrangement and the Compensatory and Contingency Facility, and by mortgaging gold to the Bank of England to raise additional resources. The emergency measures taken in April 1991 by the government included a severe compression of imports by requiring a 200 per cent cash margin on release of foreign exchange, cutting canalised imports, tightening the issue of replenishment licences to exporters, and restricting the issue of new letters of credits for capital goods imports.

In June 1991 a new government headed by Mr Narasimha Rao came to power. It initiated a programme of macroeconomic stabilization and structural adjustment to achieve, in the course of the next five years, a liberalized trade regime characterized by the absence of discretionary import licensing, and tariff rates comparable to other developing countries; an exchange rate system free of allocative restrictions for trade; and an efficient and dynamic industrial sector subject only to regulations relating to environmental security, strategic concerns, industrial safety, and unfair trading practices.[33] The IMF and World Bank were approached for supporting the programme through structural adjustment loans. As part of the reforms the rupee was devalued twice in July 1991 leading to a 20 per cent depreciation in its value. Trade policy liberalization measures were announced on 4 July which introduced a new replenishment licence system, the Exim scrip, as a principal instrument for export-related imports. Exim scrips available at a uniform rate of 30 per cent of FOB (free on board) value were to be freely tradable in the market.

A New Industrial Policy (NIP) was announced on 24 July 1991. It abolished industrial licensing in all industries irrespective of levels of investment, except in the 18 industries specified in Annex II of the Statement, which manufactured hazardous chemicals and items of elitist consumption, or impinged on national security, social well-being, or the environment. Automatic clearance for imports of capital goods up to 25 per cent of the total value of plant and equipment subject to a maximum of Rs 20 million was to be given. Phased manufacturing programmes would not be applicable to new projects.

In 34 high priority industries identified in Annex III of the Policy, foreign investment up to 51 per cent would be approved automatically provided the foreign equity inflow was sufficient to cover the cost of imported capital goods. The remittances of dividend were to be balanced by export earnings over a period of time (seven years from the commencement of production). Foreign equity proposals did not necessarily need to be accompanied by foreign technology agreements. Trading companies engaged primarily in export activities would be allowed up to 51 per cent foreign equity. A Special Empowered Board would be constituted to negotiate with large international firms and approve FDI in select areas.

The NIP also accorded automatic permission to foreign technology collaborations in high priority industries specified in Annex III up to a lumpsum payment of Rs 10 million; 5 per cent royalty for domestic sales and 8 per cent for exports subject to a total payment of 8 per cent (net of taxes) of sales over a 10 year period from the date of agreement or 7 years from commencement. No permission would be needed for hiring foreign technicians or foreign testing of indigenously developed technologies.[34] The requirement of prior approval of the government for establishment of new undertakings, effecting expansion, amalgamation, etc., under the MRTP Act was eliminated.

To implement various provisions of the NIP, the government subsequently issued guidelines and procedures for approvals of foreign investment.[35] To attract MNEs to the energy sector, 100 per cent foreign equity was permitted in the power sector.[36] International companies were allowed to explore non-associated natural gas, develop gas fields, including laying down pipelines, and set up liquified petroleum gas projects. Earlier they were allowed to develop gas associated with oil exploration.[37] A new package for 100 per cent EOUs and units in EPZs was announced including automatic clearance for proposals fulfilling the specified parameters on capital goods imports, location, value addition, etc.[38]

A Foreign Investment Promotion Board (FIPB) headed by the principal secretary to the prime minister was set up to invite and facilitate investment in India by international companies. The FIPB was authorized to provide a single window clearance for all project proposals considered by it.[39] The FIB along with its subcommittees was abolished.

In October 1991, the government allowed up to 100 per cent equity ownership by NRIs and overseas corporate bodies (OCBs) predominantly owned by them in high priority industries (as specified in the NIP of July 1991) with repatriation benefits provided equity inflow covered capital goods imports, and dividend remittances were balanced for seven years.[40] The government also issued procedures for raising foreign equity levels to 51 per cent by existing companies either operating or proposing expansion in priority industries.[41] The limit in respect of capital goods imports under the TDF was raised further in December 1991 to Rs 50 million.[42]

In another major relaxation in January 1992 the government decided to allow the use of foreign brand names for goods manufactured by the domestic industry. The existing companies could also switch over to foreign brand names from hybrid names with government permission.[43] Curbs on FERA companies were also lifted and they were allowed to open branches, permit use of their trademarks, carry out any activity of a trading, commercial or industrial nature, borrow money, and accept fixed deposits like any other Indian company.[44]

Partial convertibility of the rupee on the trade account was introduced in the 1992–93 budget as a step towards full convertibility which would be achieved in two years. Under the Liberalized Exchange Rate Management System (LERMS), 60 per cent of export earnings were to be converted at the market determined exchange rate and 40 per cent were to be bought by the government at the official exchange rate. The New Export-Import Policy for the period 1992 to 1997 was announced on 31 March 1992 which further liberalized the international trade regime. The negative lists of imports and exports were pruned further. Barring a few items, capital goods and raw materials were taken out of the negative list of imports.[45]

On 13 April 1992 India signed the convention of the Multilateral Investment Guarantee Agency (MIGA) for protection of foreign investments.[46] In the same month, foreign investors in the power sector were permitted to draw upon financial resources from Indian financial institutions to the extent of 40 per cent of their total funds requirement.[47]

In June 1992 revised procedures for raising foreign equity in existing companies were issued which liberalized the share valuation procedure to be followed while issuing new equity shares to foreign investors. The dividend balancing clause was withdrawn on all foreign investment approvals except for 22 specified consumer goods industries.[48] In July 1992, conditions imposed on letters of intent and industrial licences granted before the NIP (1991), such as those concerning export obligations, foreign exchange neutrality, and prohibition of access to domestic financial institutions were withdrawn.[49] In August

1992 the oil majors were offered 51 per cent ownership in joint ventures set up for development of known oil-fields.[50]

In September 1992 the government announced guidelines for investments by foreign institutional investors (FIIs) in the Indian capital market. FIIs were now welcome to invest in all types of securities traded on the primary and secondary market with full repatriation benefits and without restrictions on either volume of trading or lock-in period.[51] The guidelines were further liberalized in November 1992 to permit FIIs to apply for shares from quotas reserved for Indian mutual funds, NRIs, financial institutions, and employees.[52]

In October 1992, the government issued new guidelines for investments by Indian enterprises in joint ventures and wholly owned subsidiaries abroad introducing automatic approval for total Indian investments up to US $2 million out of which up to $0.5 million could be in cash.[53] In January 1993 the government promulgated an ordinance amending FERA (1973) to remove the restrictions on acquiring and holding immovable property in India or setting up joint ventures abroad by FERA companies. The ordinance, led to the deletion of Section 27 relating to restrictions on persons resident in India associating with or participating in concerns outside India. Section 29 regarding restrictions on establishment of places of business in India was amended exempting FERA companies from the prohibition on the establishment of a branch or liaison office even when the non-resident interest in such a company exceeded 40 per cent. Companies with more than 40 per cent foreign equity were now treated at par with fully Indian owned companies.[54] In January 1993 itself a package of financial sector reforms was announced that included permission to new private sector, including foreign joint ventures, banks to operate.[55]

The 1993–94 budget further reduced tariff rates on a number of items and made the rupee fully convertible. A new Mineral Policy was announced in March 1993 to allow private—including foreign—participation in the mining of 13 minerals till then reserved exclusively for the public sector. The policy raised the ceiling on foreign equity participation in Indian mining companies to 50 per cent. Minerals open for private sector investment now included iron ore, manganese, chrome, sulphur, gold, diamond, copper, lead, zinc, molybdenum, tungsten, nickel and the platinum group. Mineral and metal processing units that wished to develop captive mines to secure assured supplies of raw materials were allowed foreign equity participation in the manner and to the extent already permitted to such processing units. Equity participation of over 50 per cent by foreign parties in non-captive mines would also be considered on a case to case basis.[56]

On 31 March 1993 the government modified the Export-Import Policy (1992–97) to provide incentives for agricultural exports and trade in services. Under this scheme units engaged in agriculture, aquaculture, animal husbandry, floriculture, horticulture, pisciculture, poultry and sericulture could avail of the benefits of duty-free imports as an EOU or EPZ unit provided they exported 50 per cent of their production. Certain inputs and materials required by the agricultural sector were removed from the negative list of imports in order to make them freely importable. In the services sector, companies rendering professional consultancy services, hotels, travel agents and diagnostic centres could also import capital equipment at a concessional duty of 15 per cent if they had part of their earnings in foreign exchange, like agricultural units. Further, 144 items were dropped from the negative list of exports. The criteria for recognition of export/trading/star trading houses and value addition norms for EOU/EPZ units were also modified. In April 1993 the licensing policy was further liberalized and the government delicensed the manufacture of motor cars, white goods, like refrigerators, airconditioners and washing machines, and raw hides, skins, and patent leather. With this the number of industries requiring compulsory licensing was reduced from 18 to 15. The Budget of February 1994 further reduced custom tariffs from a peak rate of 85 per cent to 65 per cent and corporate tax rates. The rupee was made convertible on the current account. In April 1994, the government offered identified highways and bridges to the private sector including foreign investors, to build, maintain and operate on toll collection basis.[57] In May 1994 the government announced its intention to allow private including foreign companies to operate telephone service networks in the country.[58]

This liberalization of policies has been accompanied by active courting of foreign investors at the highest levels. The Prime Minister addressed a meeting of French Commerce and Industry in November 1991.[59] In February 1992 he addressed a plenary at the annual meeting of the World Economic Forum in Davos.[60] The Finance Minister addressed the Tokyo Chamber of Commerce and Industry in April 1992 and a meeting in Bonn in December 1992.[61] The Minister of State for Commerce visited the United States in September 1991 and April 1992 and addressed a meeting on investing in India organized by the World Economic Forum in Geneva in May 1992.[62] The Indian Embassy in Singapore organized an investment promotion seminar in August 1992 jointly with the Singapore Manufacturers Association.[63] In November 1992 a joint delegation of the Indian Merchants Chamber and the Associated Chamber of Commerce and Industry visited Japan and South Korea on a Promote India campaign.[64]

India also received a number of delegations of potential foreign investors. In September 1991 a team from leading MNEs of Japan, USA, Australia and the EC visited India to study the impact of recent policy changes under the auspices of the Global Leadership Programme.[65] In October 1992 a delegation of European Round Table of Industrialists comprising 40 European industrial leaders visited India.[66] In January 1993 a delegation of British industry and in February 1993 an OPIC mission visited India.[67]

An indicator of the changed Indian environment is the fact that two giants that left the country following restrictions placed on them under FERA, viz., IBM and Coca Cola, have both come back recently. IBM has set up a joint venture with the Tata group and Coca Cola has taken over the local soft drinks manufacturer, Parle.

Government Policy and Trends in Foreign Investments and Collaborations

The above discussion suggests that the Government of India has been pursuing a selective policy towards foreign collaborations and investment. The degree of selectivity has, however, changed over time. The variations in policy are reflected in the trends and patterns of FDI in India and on the approvals of foreign collaborations.

Foreign Direct Investments in India: Magnitude and Distribution

In mid-1948, when the first survey of India's international assets and liabilities was undertaken by the RBI, the stock of foreign investment in the country stood at Rs 2,560 million, and was mostly of British origin. Bulk of this FDI was concentrated in export-oriented raw materials, extractive and service sectors. Tea plantations and jute accounted for a little over a quarter of the total FDI which together contributed half of India's exports; about 32 per cent was in trading and other services, 9 per cent in petroleum, and only about 20 per cent in manufacturing other than jute (Kidron 1965: 3). By 1990, the latest year for which comparable official estimates are available, the stock of FDI in India had gone up to Rs 27,050 million (RBI 1993). Not only the magnitude but the sectoral composition, sources, and organizational forms of investment have undergone considerable changes over this period.

Table 1.1 summarizes the sectoral distribution of the stocks of FDI as at the end of the financial years 1964, 1974, 1980, and 1990. The most fundamental trend is the increasing importance of the manufacturing sector—from about a quarter of the FDI stock at the time of Independence and 40 per cent in 1964, to nearly 85 per cent in 1990. This jump has been at the cost of plantations, mining, petroleum, and services.

In all the non-manufacturing sectors the absolute volume of FDI as well as its share in the total stock declined during the period 1964 to 1980. Since 1980, however, plantations and services have marginally improved their share. Almost all the inflows of FDI to the country after 1964 were directed to the manufacturing sector, while disinvestment took place in other sectors. Though the total stock of FDI in the country stagnated during the late 1970s, in the manufacturing sector it steadily increased. This significant reorganization in the sectoral pattern of FDI in the country was stimulated by the government's selective policy. A few major nationalizations in the non-manufacturing sectors also contributed to it. Fourteen major banks, including one foreign owned, viz., the Allahabad Bank (Standard Chartered Group), were nationalized in 1969. The

Table 1.1
Sectoral Distribution of the Stock of FDI in India, 1964–1990
(Rs Crores = 10 million)

Industry group	*March 1964*		*March 1974*		*March 1980*		*March 1990*	
	Value	*%*	*Value*	*%*	*Value*	*%*	*Value*	*%*
I. Plantations	105.9	18.7	107.2	11.7	38.5	4.1	256	9.5
II. Mining	4.7	0.9	6.4	0.8	7.8	0.8	8	0.3
III. Petroleum	143.3	25.3.	137.9	14.7	36.8	3.9	3	0.1
IV. Manufacturing	229.3	40.5	625.6	68.4	811.6	86.9	2298	84.9
1. Food and beverages	30.2	13.2	52.1	8.3	39.1	4.8	162	7.0
2. Textile products	16.6	7.2	35.6	5.7	32.0	3.9	92	4.0
3. Machinery & machine tools	15.7	6.8	42.1	6.7	71.0	8.8	354	15.4
4. Transport equipment	15.0	6.5	32.1	5.1	51.5	6.3	282	12.3
5. Metal & metal products	33.1	14.4	86.7	13.9	118.7	14.6	141	6.1
6. Electrical goods	18.2	7.9	68.1	10.9	97.5	12.0	295	12.8
7. Chemicals & allied products	60.1	26.2	203.7	32.6	301.8	37.2	769	33.4
a. Chemicals	16.3	7.1	76.0	12.2	130.6	16.1	n.a.	n.a.
b. Medicines and pharmaceuticals	23.2	10.9	69.7	11.1	105.7	13.0	n.a.	n.a.
c. Others	20.6	8.9	58.1	9.3	65.5	8.1	n.a.	n.a.
8. Miscellaneous	40.4	17.6	105.0	16.7	100.0	12.3	203	8.8
V. Services	82.3	14.6	39.8	4.4	38.5	4.1	140	5.2
Total	565.5	100.0	916.9	100.0	933.2	100.0	2,705	100.0

Sources: Compiled from RBI, 'India's international investment position', *Reserve Bank of India Bulletin*: July 1975, March 1978, December 1984, and April 1985; and RBI, 'India's Foreign Liabilities and Assets As on March 31, 1989', *Reserve Bank of India Bulletin*, August 1993, pp. 1031–1051.

Note: Percentages given in manufacturing sub-sectors 1 to 8 represent the break-up of FDI in manufacturing.

general insurance companies, a number of which were British controlled, were nationalized in 1971. Petroleum investments were nationalized between 1974 and 1976. In plantations, most of the FCEs were foreign branches which were obliged under FERA to Indianize themselves. The share of manufacturing in the total FDI stock in India was favourable even when compared to the sectoral distribution of the total flow of FDI to developing countries. Thus, while manufacturing accounted for only 32, 64 and 42 per cent respectively of all American (1979–1981), British (1971–1978), and Japanese (1951–1980) FDI in developing countries (UNCTC 1983), it accounted for 87 percent of the FDI stock in India.

Within the manufacturing sector, the new investments were directed at technology-intensive sectors, such as electrical goods, transport equipment, machinery and machine tools, and chemical and allied products (in particular, chemicals, medicines and pharmaceuticals). These four broad sectors accounted for nearly 74 per cent of total FDI in manufacturing in 1990 in contrast to 47.4 per cent in 1964. The rising importance of technology-intensive products in FDI stock was at the expense of traditional industries, such as food and beverages, textile products, and metal and metal products. As a result of the liberal policies of the 1980s, however, consumer goods industries, such as food and beverages, and textile products have also marginally improved their share in manufacturing FDI.

Table 1.2
Organizational Distribution of FDI in India, 1964–1990
(Rs crores = 10 million)

Year	*Foreign Branches*		*Foreign Controlled Rupee Companies (FCRC)*		*Total*
	Value	*%*	*Majority owned*	*Minority owned*	
1964	259.7	45.92	239.9 (42.42)	65.9 (11.65)	565.5 (100.0)
1974	241.6	26.45	470.4 (51.50)	201.4 (22.05)	913.4 (100.0)
1980	60.4	6.47	454.6 (48.71)	418.2 (44.81)	933.2 (100.0)
1990*	54.1	2.00	2,650.9 (98.0)		2,705 (100.0)

Source: See Table 1.1
*Estimated share on the basis of distribution for 1989.

Similar restructuring took place in the organizational form of FDI. In 1964, foreign branches accounted for 45.92 per cent of India's FDI liability (see Table 1.2). By 1990, their share had fallen to a mere 2.0 per cent of FDI stock. Among the companies registered in India (i.e., FCRCs), the trend was also one of increasing minority ownership. In 1964, only 11.65 per cent of FDI was held in the minority FCRCs, their proportion increased to about 45 per cent by 1980. These trends in the organizational form of FDI—the decline in branches and the increasing acceptance of minority ownership by foreign investors—was the outcome of government policy, in particular FERA.

There has also been a geographical diversification in the sources of FDI in India over the last three decades. A considerable erosion of the dominance of the UK as a source of FDI has occurred (see Table 1.3). In 1964 its share was nearly 77 per cent; by 1990 it had fallen to about 49 per cent. The US has emerged as a major source of FDI, improving its share from 14.5 per cent in 1964 to 19 per cent in 1990. Germany, Switzerland, Japan, Sweden and Canada, have also become significant sources of FDI to India. Germany accounted for nearly 10 per cent of the FDI stock in 1990 compared to just 1.13 per cent in 1964. Japan increased its share from 0.46 per cent to 4.9 per cent in the 1980s.

Table 1.3

Home Country-wise Distribution of FDI, 1964–1990

(Rs crores = 10 million)

Home Country	*1964*		*1980*		*1990*	
	FDI	*%*	*FDI*	*%*	*FDI*	*%*
UK	433.0	76.57	503.3	53.93	1321	48.8
USA	82.3	14.53	196.4	21.04	518	19.1
Germany	6.4	1.13	65.0	6.96	267	9.9
Japan	n.a.	n.a.	4.3	0.46	132	4.9
Sweden	7.8	1.38	20.1	2.15	77	2.8
Switzerland	13.6	2.40	54.7	5.86	86	3.2
Canada	8.7	1.50	34.1	3.65	76	2.8
The Netherlands	n.a.	n.a.	n.a.	n.a.	36	1.3

Source: See Table 1.1

Foreign Collaboration Approvals

The changing attitude of the government towards foreign investment and technology is reflected in the number of foreign collaborations approved in different periods. Table 1.4 summarizes three indicators for different periods; (*a*) average number of foreign collaborations approved per year; (*b*) proportion of foreign collaborations with equity participation; and (*c*) the volume of foreign investment approved. The variations in these parameters across time reveal the nature of the change in government policy. The gradual liberalization of policy in the early post-Independence period in the wake of the economic crisis of the late 1950s resulted in an almost five-fold increase in the number of collaborations approved per year—from 50 during the period 1948-1958 to 297 during 1959-1966. Since foreign exchange was the major constraint during the period, a high (over 36 per cent) proportion of the collaborations approved were with financial participation. The restrictive posture adopted by the government during the 1967–79 period brought down the average number of approvals to 242. The squeeze on foreign financial collaborations was far more drastic, bringing their proportion down from 36.36 per cent during the period 1959-1966 to just 16.11 per cent during 1967-1979.

Table 1.4
Summary of Foreign Collaboration Approvals, 1948–1993

		Those with foreign equity		
Period	*Average no. of collaborations approved per year*	*Average no. per year*	*Proportion in total*	*Average foreign investment involved per year (Rs million)*
1948–58	50	n.a.	n.a.	n.a.
1959–66	297	108*	36.36	n.a.
1967–79	242	39	16.11	53.62
1980–88	744	170	22.80	930.84
1989–90	635	194	30.55	2,224.95
1991–93	1,315	589	44.76	44,280.40

* On the basis of 1961 to 1966

Source: See Table 1.1.

The considerable liberalization of policy in the 1980s caused the average number of approvals per year to increase from 242 during the period 1967–1979 to 744 during 1980–1988. The increase in the number of financial collaborations per year was even sharper, their proportion in total approvals increasing from 16.1 per cent to 22.8 per cent. The average value of foreign investments approved per year increased by over 17 times from Rs 53.62 million to Rs 930.84 million. Political instability during the period 1989–1990 seems to have brought the average number of approvals down from 744 to 635 per year. The number of approvals involving financial participation as well as foreign investment, however, were considerably higher than in the preceding period. Following the announcement of the New Industrial Policy (July 1991) the number of approvals jumped to 950 in 1991 (of which 634 were recorded in the last four months of the year) and to 1,476 in just 10 months of 1993 (See Table 1.5). The rise in collaborations involving financial participation was even sharper and their proportion in total collaborations (viz., 44.76) crossed that achieved during 1959–1966 (See Table 1.4). The average foreign investment approvals in the 1991–93 period shows a quantum jump from Rs 2.2 billion a year in the previous period to Rs 44.2 billion. The liberalization of policy since July 1991 appears to have considerably improved the investment climate in the country for the foreign investors. The actual inflow of FDI, however, has been much smaller at Rs 28 billion in the three year period 1991–93, due perhaps to gestation lags involved in projects. Another significant trend is that the non-resident Indians are emerging as significant investors in the country after liberalization. They accounted for 11.3 per cent of actual inflows of FDI during the 1991–93 period.

Concluding Remarks

In sum, government policy towards foreign collaborations has been marked by a selective attitude throughout much of the post-Independence period with significant variations in intensity over time. An elaborate system of entry regulations and guidelines for foreign collaborators has evolved. The selectivity

Table 1.5
Foreign Collaboration Approvals, 1948–1993

Year	*Total number of cases approved*	*Cases involving foreign capital participation*	*Foreign investment involved (Rs million)*
1948–55	284	n.a.	n.a.
1956	82	n.a.	n.a.
1957	81	n.a.	n.a.
1958	103	n.a.	n.a.
1959	150	n.a.	n.a.
1960	380	n.a.	n.a.
1961	403	165	n.a.
1962	298	124	n.a.
1963	298	115	n.a.
1964	403	123	n.a.
1965	241	71	n.a.
1966	202	49	n.a.
1967	182	62	n.a.
1968	131	30	n.a.
1969	134	29	n.a.
1970	183	32	24.52
1971	245	46	58.38
1972	257	37	62.27
1973	265	34	28.17
1974	359	55	67.13
1975	271	40	32.05
1976	277	39	72.69
1977	267	27	40.03
1978	307	44	94.06
1979	267	32	56.87
1980	526	73	89.24
1981	389	57	108.71
1982	592	113	628.10
1983	673	129	618.10
1984	752	151	1,130.00
1985	1,024	239	1,258.70
1986	957	240	1,069.52
1987	853	242	1,077.05
1988	926	282	2,387.50
1989	605	193	3,166.70
1990	666	194	1,283.2
1991	950	289	5,341.2
1992	1,520	692	38,900.0
1993	1,476	785	88,600.0

Source: Government of India, Ministry of Industry, Department of Scientific and Industrial Research, *Annual Report 1992*; Government of India, Indian Investment Centre, *Economic Survey 1992–93*; Government of India, *SIA Newsletter*, March 1994.

of policy has guided the bulk of new FDI inflows to technology-intensive areas in manufacturing, and has encouraged minority foreign ownership in Indian companies. The recent liberalization has brought about a considerable change in the posture of the government towards FDIs from one of passive approver of the proposals to an active seeker. This change in attitude deserves a comment in the light of the policy goals and empirical findings. This is attempted in the Postscript.

Notes

1. For a detailed analysis of the evolution of government policy up to the early 1960s see Kidron (1965, chs. 3 and 4).
2. See the Swadeshi Resolution of the Federation of Indian Chambers of Commerce and Industry, which was adopted in 1953.
3. Government of India, press note, 8 May 1961; cf. the earlier position of preferring local majority ownership.
4. Government of India, press note, 20 July 1968, and the announcement of the Government of India on 27 November 1968.
5. The Act replaced the Patents Act of 1911.
6. Government of India, press note, 19 February 1972.
7. Government of India, 'Guidelines for licensing of items reserved for small-scale sector and entry of large/foreign houses in non-core industries,' and 'Industrial Policy: Government Decisions,' February 1973.
8. Foreign branches are defined in the Indian Companies Act as enterprises which are incorporated abroad but have a place of business in India.
9. The Industrial licensing policy restricts the expansion of local large and foreign companies in non-core industries; see note 7.
10. See the list of FERA companies, and replies to Lok Sabha unstarred question no. 4921, 18 September 1981.
11. See replies to Lok Sabha unstarred questions nos. 2100 and 2214, 9 March 1984.
12. For instance, 72 companies diluted their foreign equity even before specific FERA directives were issued to them. Another 54 companies which were permitted to retain over 40 per cent foreign equity volunteered to dilute to 40 per cent. See Lok Sabha question no. 4921, September 1981.
13. See, for instance, Government of India, Ministry of Commerce, Committee on Export Strategy (Tandon Committee), New Delhi, 1980.
14. *ibid.*
15. See *Multinational Business*, No. 3 (1985: 10–17).
16. See *Business America*, 7 February 1983.
17. See *The Hindustan Times*, 1 June 1981.
18. See *Financial Express*, 20 January 1987.
19. Government of India, Industrial Policy Statement, July 1980.
20. *The Economic Times*, 10 December 1986.

21. *India Today*, 31 December 1988; 121.
22. Ministry of Industry press note no. 2 (1)/89–TDF, 17 March 1989.
23. *Business Standard*, 31 May 1988.
24. *Monthly Newsletter-Indian Investment Centre*, October 1989.
25. *Business America, op. cit.*
26. *India Today, op. cit.*
27. *Monthly Newsletter-Indian Investment Centre*, February, March, and May 1990, respectively.
28. *ibid.*, April 1990.
29. *ibid.*, June 1990.
30. *The Economic Times*, 24 December, 1990.
31. *The Hindustan Times*, 9 October 1990, 28 March 1991, 1 June 1991 respectively.
32. Government of India, Ministry of Finance, *Economic Survey, 1991-1992*. New Delhi.
33. The letter of the Finance Minister dated 11 November 1991 to the President of the world Bank enclosing a note on the Programme for Structural Reform, as reproduced in the *Reserve Bank of India Bulletin*, April 1992: 779–91.
34. *Monthly Newsletter-Indian Investment Centre*, July 1991.
35. *Vide* Ministry of Industry, Dept. of Industrial Development, Press notes, 14 August, 20 August, and 31 August 1991; and Reserve Bank of India press release Nos. 1991–92/94, 10 and 14 September 1991.
36. *Business and Political Observer*, 29 August 1991.
37. *The Economic Times*, 30 August 1991.
38. Statement tabled in Parliament on 13 August 1991 and Ministry of Industry press notes, 26 September and 9 October 1991.
39. Ministry of Industry, press note, 22 August 1991.
40. Ministry of Finance (Dept. of Economic Affairs) press note, 28 October 1991.
41. Ministry of Industry, press note, 19 November 1991.
42. *Monthly Newsletter-Indian Investment Centre*, December 1991.
43. *The Economic Times*, 3 January 1992; also see Government of India press note No. 6, 14 May 1992.
44. *The Economic Times*, 30 January 1992.
45. *Monthly Newsletter-Indian Investment Centre*, April 1992.
46. *Monthly Newsletter-Indian Investment Centre*, May 1992.
47. *The Economic Times*, 25 April 1992.
48. Ministry of Industry, press notes, 26 and 29 June 1992.
49. Ministry of Industry, press note, 28 July 1992.
50. *The Economic Times*, 23 August 1992.
51. Ministry of Finance (Dept. of Economic Affairs), press note, 14 September 1992.
52. *The Economic Times*, 5 November 1992.
53. *Monthly Newsletter-Indian Investment Centre*, November 1992.
54. *The Hindustan Times*, 9 January 1993.
55. *International Herald Tribune*, 3 May 1993.
56. *The Hindustan Times*, 6 March 1993.
57. *International Herald Tribune*, 26 April 1994.
58. *International Herald Tribune*, 14-15 May, 1994.
59. *Financial Express*, 26 November 1991.

60. *The Economic Times*, 4 February 1992; *Business India*, 14-27 February 1994.
61. *The Hindustan Times*, 11 April 1992 and *The Economic Times*, 6 December 1992.
62. *The Hindustan Times*, 9 April 1992 and *The Economic Times*, 27 September 1991 and 16 May 1992.
63. *The Economic Times*, 4 August 1992.
64. *The Economic Times*, 11 November 1992.
65. *Business and Political Observer*, 3 September 1991.
66. *The Hindustan Times*, 2 October 1992.
67. *The Hindustan Times*, 27 January and 3 February 1993 respectively.
68. *SIA Newsletter*, Government of India, Ministry of Industry (Secretariat of Industrial Approvals) March 1994.

2

Foreign Enterprises in Indian Industry: Overall and Sectoral Shares

Introduction

Though it is generally accepted that multinational affiliates or FCEs have an important place in the industrial economy of India, there exist few precise estimates of their shares, particularly at the disaggregated level. This situation has hampered any rigorous analysis of the pattern of their operation and their impact on the economy. This chapter reviews the existing estimates of the economic significance of FCEs in the country and provides fresh estimates of the shares of FCEs in the industrial sector as a whole. It also presents the shares of FCEs in 54 three-digit manufacturing industries.

Importance of Foreign Controlled Enterprises: Overall Manufacturing

Existing Estimates

The absolute volume of FDI by itself does not reveal the importance of FCEs in the economy. For this, one needs to have an idea of their share in the relevant macro aggregates, such as assets or sales. A few attempts have been made in the past to estimate the importance of FCEs in the Indian economy. It has been argued that the importance of foreign capital should be judged with respect to the sectors where they operate and not in relation to the economy as a whole (Bettelheim 1968: 58: Chandra 1977). Hence, most studies estimate the relative importance of FCEs in the organized private corporate sector.

Table 2.1
Summary of Estimates of Foreign Share in Indian Industries

Estimates by:	*Reference period*	*Estimated share of FCEs (%)*	*Denominator*
Bettelheim (1968)	1953	50	Capital invested in big industries (organized)
Kurien (1966)	1948	35.8	Private corporate sector
	1960	40.4	
Kidron (1965)	1961	40	Organized or large-scale private sector
	1961	25	In modern sector as a whole
Chaudhuri (1978)	1971	42.2	Capital of stock exchange quoted companies
Chandra (1977)	1957–58 to	26.1	Sales of non-government large companies (RBI sample)
	1972–73	29.8	

Table 2.1 provides a summary view of these estimates. The estimates range from 25 per cent to 50 per cent for different periods. It is difficult to deduce trends from these estimates, as they relate to different variables, (such as capital invested, paid-up capital, sales, and profits) and use different samples, (such as the private corporate sector, the organized sector, and stock exchange quoted companies).

In the absence of systematic database Bettelheim (1968) and Kidron (1965) depended mainly on their judgement for arriving at estimates of the share of FCEs. Kurien (1966) attempted to provide a time series of the share of FCEs in the private corporate sector for the period 1948 to 1960 and found that it had increased from 35.8 per cent in 1948 to 40.4 per cent in 1960. He divided the net worth of foreign companies by the total paid-up capital of the corporate sector. This resulted in an overestimation. Chaudhuri (1978) divided the paid-up capital of all FCEs by that of companies quoted at the stock exchanges instead of the entire private corporate sector, which probably explains the high percentage (42.2 per cent) he obtained. Chandra (1977) based his estimates on the RBI's company finances studies. His time series showed an increasing trend in the share of FCEs in private corporate sector sales—from 26.1 per cent in 1957–58 to 29.8 per cent in 1972–73. The share of FCEs in private corporate sector profits computed by Chandra was much higher than their share in sales, and exhibited a similarly increasing trend. In 1972–73 FCEs enjoyed almost half of total profits of the private corporate sector in the RBI sample.

Fresh Estimates of Foreign Shares

We have attempted to update the estimates of foreign shares available in existing studies up to 1980–81. Four sets of estimates of foreign shares have been provided in Table 2.2 of which three are for two periods, that is, 1972–73 and 1980–81. Though Chandra's estimates are available for 1972–73 we have recomputed them for the sample as in 1980–81 so as to facilitate intertemporal comparisons. Though the basic source of data for these computations is the same as that of Chandra, that is, the RBI company finances studies, two differences in the coverage make these estimates mutually incomparable. First, our sample excluded small public limited companies for which RBI had not published data for some years. Second, the coverage of the RBI survey on the finances of FBs and FCRCs for the period between 1975–76 and 1980–81 might not be comparable to that of 1972–73. The surveys for the period up to 1972–73 covered select FBs and FCRCs which accounted for nearly 90 per cent of the paid-up capital of the respective populations. The recent surveys, however, do not indicate the extent of coverage. The coverage in the case of FBs appears to be particularly deficient as only eight branches are listed in 1980–81. Hence, for the first set of estimates in Table 2.2, we excluded FBs from the sample. This set, thus, shows only the share of FCRCs in sales or assets of medium and large public and private limited companies in 1972-73 and 1980–81. The second set of estimates includes FBs as covered by the RBI surveys. In the third set we have attempted to correct the coverage of FBs and FCRCs (for the years 1970 to 1980) by using additional data from the Department of Company Affairs (DCA).

Table 2.2

Estimates of Share of FCEs at Overall Industrial Level

Sample and variable	*Percentage share of FCEs*	
	1972–73	*1980–81*
1. FCRCs in medium & large non-government companies		
a. in sales	27.17	24.08
b. in assets	27.13	22.97
c. in profit before tax	45.72	34.75
2. FCRCs and FBs in medium & large non-government companies and FBs		
a. in sales	33.84	24.38
b. in assets	30.85	23.14
c. in profit before tax	49.56	36.48
3. Corrected coverage of FCRCs and FBs in medium & large non-government companies and FBs		
a. assets	30.85	25.08*
4. FCRCs in sales of medium & large non-government public limited companies in the manufacturing sector	n.a.	31.41

Source: Our computations as described in the text.

Note: * The numerator for this estimate consisted of assets in 1979–80 of non-banking FBs and Foreign Subsidiaries (FSUs) (taken from the Department of Company Affairs) and assets of minority FCRCs projected for the stock of FDI in the year on the basis of FDI to FCRC assets ratio in 1972–73 (with adjustments for change in debt-equity proportion over the period and assuming on average a 15 per cent reduction in foreign equity holdings as a result of FERA). The denominator is assets of medium and large non-government companies and non-banking foreign branches (DCA) in 1979–1980.

The DCA publishes data on assets of FBs and (majority-owned) foreign subsidiaries (FSUs). To the asset figures of non-banking FBs and FSUs as published by DCA we added the assets of minority-owned FCRCs projected on the basis of FDI in 1979–80 using the FDI to asset relationship in case of FCRCs for the year 1972–73 and making adjustments for changes in debt-equity ratio and the proportion of foreign equity held. Dividing the total foreign controlled assets thus obtained by the assets of medium and large, public and private limited companies, and non-banking FBs in 1979–80 one gets the figure of 25.08 per cent. The fourth set gives the share of FCRCs in the sales of medium and large public limited companies in manufacturing (Appendix I gives more details on data and methodology pertaining to the last set).

A look at these alternative estimates indicates that: (*a*) the foreign share in sales or assets of the larger private corporate sector was around 23 per cent in 1980–81 depending upon the coverage; (*b*) as also noted by Chandra (1977), their share in profits was much higher than in either sales or assets; (*c*) whichever sample and variable is used, the trend suggests a decline in foreign shares over the period from 1972–73 to 1980–81; and (*d*) foreign share in manufacturing is higher than in the industrial sector as a whole because of the concentration of FCEs in manufacturing.[1]

The phenomena of declining foreign shares over the 1970s (see Table 2.2) is worth noting, especially in the light of the increasing trend observed by Chandra (1977) for the preceding period (i.e., 1957–58 to 1972–73). Besides the restrictive government policy towards foreign collaboration during the 1970s, nationalization in certain sectors, such as oil and coal mining, and a few disinvestments triggered by FERA, might explain the declining foreign shares in the period. FCEs do, however, continue to be a significant and more profitable segment of the large private corporate sector in India, particularly in manufacturing.

Shares of FCEs in Individual Manufacturing Industries

The previous analysis shows that FCEs constitute a significant and prosperous segment of Indian industry. It should be emphasized, however, that MNEs mainly operate in those branches of industry where they enjoy a competitive edge over existing or potential local competitors. This implies that the industrial distribution of shares of FCEs would be uneven and hence, the estimates of their share in the overall organized sector may not reveal their true importance. For this, one has to analyse their share in individual branches of industry.

There have not been many estimates of the share of FCE at the sectoral level in Indian industry. Kurien (1966) computed shares of FCRCs in exports and imports of individual sectors at a two-digit level of disaggregation for the years 1956 and 1958, which revealed a near domination in exports of tea, tobacco, jute (yarns and manufacture); and imports of mineral oils, chemicals (including drugs), electrical goods, machinery, and transport equipment by FCEs. Kidron (1965) attempted to examine the importance of FCEs in different industries. However, his exercise could not yield precise estimates because of the lack of a systematic data base. On the basis of information collected from a variety of sources on capacities authorized or installed, he judged qualitatively whether the industry was (or was not) going to be dominated by FCEs. Kelkar (1977) presented shares of FCEs in total sales of public limited companies included in the RBI sample in seven industries where they were dominant in 1972–73. These industries were: aluminium, chemicals, engineering, rubber products, mineral oil, and tea plantations. Lall and Mohammad (1983a) computed the proportion of dividends remitted abroad in total dividends paid by the firms on the basis of finances of medium and large public limited companies published by RBI for broad industry groups. The proportion of dividends remitted, however, might not necessarily reflect the share of FCEs in industry because of (*a*) differing profitability of FCEs and local firms; (*b*) restriction on foreign equity holding to 40 per cent in India; and (*c*) dividend remittances on portfolio investments.

Foreign Shares in Individual Industries

An attempt was made to compute the shares of FCEs in sales in 54 branches of the manufacturing industry (disaggregated at the 3-digit level) for a six-year period from 1975–76 to 1980–81 on the basis of a sample of 1,334 medium and large public limited companies in the private sector (see Appendix I for details of methodology and sources). Table 2.3 presents the estimates of shares of FCEs in sales in 54 manufacturing industries for the years 1975–76 and 1980–81. Two limitations of these estimates have to be borne in mind while analysing them. First, these are based on a sample of 1,334 medium and large non-government public limited manufacturing companies. They may not reveal the true market position of FCEs in some industries where the public sector, private limited companies, or the non-corporate sector firms have considerable operations. Second, the sample size in the RBI company finance studies which we have used for computations is decided at the beginning of the quinquennial series and is kept the same for the entire series. Hence, changes in shares over the period 1975–76 to 1980–81 are outcomes of the relative rates of growth of the selected firms, and do not reflect the effect of new entries or divestments.

Table 2.3

Share of FCEs in Indian Manufacturing, 1975–76 and 1980–81 (Medium and Large Non-Government Public Limited Companies)

Code	*Industry*	*No of companies*		*FCE's share in sales (%)*	
		Total	*Foreign*	*1975–76*	*1980–81*
310	Grain and pulses mills	8	0	–	–
320	Edible oil mills	13	1	15.41	18.11
331	Sugar mills	57	0	–	–
332	Other processed foods	31	9	82.84	80.52
341	Cigarettes	6	2	85.14	78.23
342	Tobacco products, n.e.s.	2	0	–	–
351–4	Cotton textiles	238	3	6.78	5.73
355	Jute textiles	31	0	–	–
356–8	Silk and rayon textiles	13	0	–	–
359	Woollen textiles	9	0	–	–
360	Other textile products	14	1	13.68	19.23
370	Breweries and distilleries	19	1	3.96	3.04
380	Leather and products	3	1	98.21	97.94
390	Miscellaneous	25	1	0.39	0.33
410	Iron and steel mills	1	0	–	–
420	Aluminium manufacture	3	2	90.96	89.86
430	Other non-ferrous metals	8	4	45.46	36.13
441	Motor vehicles	13	3	16.96	19.45
442	Automotive components	32	12	65.99	66.07
443–4	Other transport equipment	14	2	43.95	52.21
445	Electric cables	15	3	36.45	32.01

Table 2.3 Contd.

Code	*Industry*	*No of companies*		*FCE's share in sales (%)*	
		Total	*Foreign*	*1975–76*	*1980–81*
446	Dry batteries	7	4	83.11	89.32
447	Electric lamps	7	3	62.05	63.57
448	Electrical machinery and equipment, n.e.s.	86	26	59.03	53.30
449	Machine tools	12	3	38.56	35.08
450	Textile machinery	13	2	9.52	7.26
451	Non-electrical machinery, n.e.s.	126	52	44.80	45.31
452	Steel tubes and pipes	14	4	51.89	51.16
453	Steel wire ropes	13	2	37.67	36.83
454	Steel forgings	29	2	6.04	5.05
455	Foundries and engineering workshops	43	4	8.52	7.54
456–7	Metal products, n.e.s.	40	12	74.27	69.64
461	Chemical fertilizers	13	3	46.80	37.46
462	Dyes and dyestuffs	10	3	30.32	30.57
463	Man-made fibres	13	3	18.60	17.83
464	Plastic raw materials	12	5	71.50	71.78
465	Basic industrial chemicals	43	13	55.45	53.85
466	Medicines & pharmaceuticals	52	24	72.84	71.07
467	Paints and varnishes	15	5	55.01	52.13
468	Toiletries and other chemicals	47	20	70.73	72.11
470	Safety matches	1	1	100.00	100.00
521	Cement	15	2	6.37	5.24
522	Asbestos and asbestos products	4	2	46.18	43.78
531–2	Ceramics and structural clay products	19	1	3.08	3.92
541	Tyres/tubes	6	3	69.40	60.13
542	Other rubber products	14	2	12.49	13.55
551	Paper	25	1	3.35	3.95
552	Products of paper and board	16	1	5.33	6.76
553	Wood products and furniture	15	1	3.15	3.14
561	Glass containers	6	1	19.18	8.08
562	Other glass products	6	3	52.34	50.78
580	Plastic products	15	2	24.31	18.01
630	Industrial and medical gases	11	1	66.92	63.13
590	Miscellaneous	32	8	26.99	32.30
	Manufacturing	1,334	262	32.78	31.41

Source: Our computations as described in the text.
Note: n.e.s. indicates not elsewhere specified.

The shares vary widely across industries in a range between 0 and 100. For ease in analysis, foreign share will be considered low in the percentage range 0 to 33; medium, in the range 34 to 66; and high if it is over 66 per cent. If this admittedly arbitrary classification is followed then 11 industries find a place in the high foreign share category in 1980–81; these include processed food products, cigarettes, leather and leather products, aluminium, automotive components, dry batteries, metal products (other than machinery and machine tools), plastic raw materials, medicines and pharmaceuticals, toilet preparations and other chemical products, and safety matches. However, foreign shares in the case of leather products and safety matches are misleading since these industries are now reserved for the small-scale sector. FCEs which had established themselves, namely, Bata and Wimco (Swedish Match) respectively before the reservation, compete mostly with local small-scale firms. In the case of aluminium, plastic raw materials, as well as medicines and pharmaceuticals, the share of FCEs is overestimated because the public sector has a significant presence in each of them.

The 15 industries where foreign shares are in the medium range include non-ferrous basic metals other than aluminium, transport equipment other than vehicles, electric lamps, electrical machinery and appliances, machine tools, other non-electrical machinery, steel tubes and pipes, steel wire ropes, fertilizers, basic industrial chemicals, paints and varnishes, asbestos cement and asbestos cement products, sheet and speciality glass, automobile tyres and tubes, industrial and medical gases. Again, these shares may be overestimates particularly in the case of non-ferrous basic metals (other than aluminium), machinery (electrical and non-electrical), machine tools, and fertilizers, due to the presence of the public sector. Among the industries where foreign share is less than one-third, FCEs have a significant presence (over 10 per cent share) in nine industries, namely, edible oils, automobiles, electric cables, dyes and dyestuff, man-made fibres, rubber products other than tyres, plastic products, and other textile products including ginning and pressing. FCEs hold marginal (less than 10 per cent) shares in 12 industries: cotton textiles, breweries and distilleries, textile machinery, steel forgings, foundries, cement, ceramics and structural clay products, paper, products of paper and board, wood products, and glass containers. They have absolutely no representation in the remaining seven industries: grain and pulses mills, sugar, tobacco other than cigarettes, textiles (jute, silk and rayon, wool), and iron and steel.

It may be pointed out that even the three-digit industry classification in some industrial classes is quite aggregative and does not represent the true market position. For instance, electrical and non-electrical machinery industries comprise several highly specialized and heterogeneous sub-branches of equipment. An analysis based on a more detailed classification may thus reveal that FCEs are concentrated some of them; for instance, in the non-electrical machinery sector they are concentrated in heavy diesel engines, pumps and compressors, cigarette-making machinery, rubber machinery, ball bearings, lifts, water treatment plants, industrial valves, abrasives, etc.

Foreign shares, had a tendency to decline over the period between 1975–76 and 1980–81 in most cases (see Table 2.3). The most significant decline is evident in industries, such as cigarettes, non-ferrous metal manufactures (other than aluminium), fertilizers, automobile tyres and tubes, glass containers, and plastic products. The industries where foreign shares have increased are motor vehicles, automotive components, transport equipment other than vehicles, dry batteries, toiletries and other chemicals, electric lamps, rubber products (other than tyres and tubes), and paper and paper products. These changes, however, do not reflect the influence of new investments, nor of divestments.

The importance of FCEs in a number of industries has undergone considerable change since the early 1960s, the period to which Kidron's (1965) analysis relates. Kidron had observed the government's tendency to curb the market power of FCEs wherever they appeared to exercise 'unchallenged control' by pushing public or local private sector firms into competition. Thus, giant public sector firms have entered high technology fields such as non-ferrous basic metals, fertilizers, heavy organic chemicals, petrochemicals, basic drugs, heavy electrical, and non-electrical machinery. Local private firms have made inroads into the market share of FCEs in edible and hydrogenated oils, automobile tyres and tubes, industrial and medical gases, and various branches of industrial machinery and equipment. The erosion of importance of FCEs in traditional industries, like jute, cotton textiles, paper, cement, and sugar, which had set in in the 1950s and 1960s, is now more or less complete.[2] FCEs, however, continue to hold large market shares in a number of industries producing consumer goods sold under brand names, such as processed foods, cigarettes, toiletries, and leather goods. This could be explained in terms of consumer loyalty enjoyed by the FCE brands.

Conclusion

This chapter examined the place of FCEs in Indian industry in terms of their shares in industry sales, assets, and profits. Previous estimates of the share of FCEs in sales and assets of the organized private corporate sector have ranged between 25 and 50 per cent depending upon the sample used and the reference period. According to our calculations, their share in sales or assets of the organized private corporate sector was nearly 23 per cent in 1980–81. Their share shows a declining tendency over the period between 1972–73 and 1980–81. The shares of FCEs in 54 industries were also computed. These were found to vary widely across industries. An analysis of characteristics of industries with high foreign shares is reserved for a detailed treatment in chapter 3.

Notes

1. Chandra (1991: 684) updated our estimates of the share of FBs and FCRCs in private corporate sector sales for the year 1984–85. According to his computations the average foreign share in private corporate sector sales for the years 1982–83 to 1984–85 was 18.2 per cent compared to 24.38 per cent in 1980–81 according to our computations. He concluded that the trend of declining importance of foreign enterprises observed by us 'remain true up to 1984–85.'
2. Encarnation (1989: 8) has explained the systematic decline in foreign share in most industries by 1981 as resulting from sequential steps taken by host country institutions, that is, mobilizing necessary finance, employing finance to acquire requisite technology, and finally combining finance and technology to control domestic markets.

3

Determinants of Foreign Shares in Indian Manufacturing: A Test of the Internalization Theory

Introduction

Chapter 2 provided estimates of the shares of FCEs in industry sales (foreign shares or FS). The distribution of foreign shares is highly uneven across different branches of manufacturing. The intangible assets theory of FDI (Hymer 1960 published in 1976; Kindleberger 1969; and Caves 1971, 1974a) and its various extensions (Dunning 1979; Rugman 1981) predict an uneven inter-industry distribution dependent upon the existence of ownership and internalization advantages. It is not known, however, whether the pattern observed in India's case is explicable in terms of predictions emanating from these theories. A number of studies have examined the determinants of foreign shares in other countries, beginning with the pioneering study by Caves (1974a) for Canada and the United Kingdom; Caves *et al*. (1980), Saunders (1982), Owen (1982), Gupta (1983) also for Canada; and Lall and Siddharthan (1982) for the United States.[1] The only study of this kind for India is by Lall and Mohammad (1983a) who analysed variations in the proportion of dividends remitted abroad in total dividends paid (and not foreign share in sales) across broad industry groups. Non-availability of estimates of foreign shares could be one of the reasons for the lack of studies on India.

Most of these studies explaining foreign shares have used the framework of the intangible assets hypothesis. Dunning (1983) has argued that possession of intangible assets alone could not explain FDI in the period following the late 1960s as arm's length licensing[2] emerged as an important alternative. Thus, according to the more recent propositions, FDI would be a preferred mode of foreign production only if the external markets of intangible assets in question are subject to high transaction costs and hence internalization incentives are present (Buckley and Casson 1976; Dunning 1981, ch. 4; Rugman 1981). In other cases licensing may be the prime modality. FDI in host countries should, therefore, be concentrated in those branches of industry where intangible assets characterized by high transaction costs provide a competitive edge to the owning firm. If assets with relatively low transaction costs are the source of competitive edge, licensing would be the preferred mode of foreign involvement in the industry. A rigorous test of these predictions has, perhaps, been constrained by problems involved in classifying intangible assets between those with high and low internalization incentives.[3]

This chapter analyses the determinants of foreign shares and licensing in Indian manufacturing industries in the framework of recent theoretical propositions. It begins by adapting the contemporary theory of foreign operations of firms to a simpler, testable form. It then attempts to classify intangible assets on the basis of relative transaction costs, and formulates testable hypotheses. Finally, it empirically examines how far these hypotheses are able to explain inter-industry variation in the intensities of FDI (the foreign shares) and licensing in Indian manufacturing.

Theory and Hypotheses

According to the intangible assets approach of horizontal foreign expansion of firms[4] originally put forward by Hymer (1960, published 1976), Kindleberger (1969) and Caves (1971, 1974a), a firm operating abroad must possess advantages adequate enough to more than offset the handicaps faced in an alien atmosphere and to cover the greater risks. These advantages are sometimes referred to as monopolistic advantages and emanate from the *ownership* of proprietary intangible assets possessed by firms, such as brand goodwill, technology (patented or otherwise), managerial and marketing skills, access to cheaper sources of capital, and raw materials. In the first phase of the 'product cycle' the advantages are exploited abroad through exports from the country of origin (Vernon 1966). In the second phase local production through FDI is undertaken because *locational* advantages, which make it more profitable than exports, begin to emerge.[5] These advantages arise from factors, such as tariffs and quantitative restrictions imposed on imports by host countries, communication and transport costs, and inter-country differences in input/factor prices and productivity. FDI should, therefore, be concentrated in those branches of manufacturing where intangible assets complemented by locational factors are important.

Due to imperfections in the market for knowledge, ownership and locational advantages usually provided sufficient conditions for FDI flows during the early post-war period. In the period following the late 1960s, however, the standardization of a wide variety of technologies, and hence, increasing competition coupled with improved bargaining position of host country governments, provided arm's length licensing of intangible assets as an alternative to FDI (Dunning 1983).[6] Mere ownership of intangible assets and the presence of locational advantages were no longer sufficient (though they were still necessary) conditions for FDI. These developments, therefore, led to a new stream of theorizing that made ownership, locational, and *internalization* advantages, necessary and sufficient conditions for FDI. After the initial proposition by McManus (1972), and Buckley and Casson (1976), the internalization approach[7] has been enriched by the contributions of Dunning (1979, 1981, ch. 4), Magee (1977), Rugman (1981), Teece (1981, 1983), Williamson (1981), Caves (1982), and Hennart (1982).

The internalization approach draws from the market failure and information asymmetry hypotheses of Coase (1937), Arrow

(1962), and Williamson (1975). The (external) markets for intangible assets are often inefficient channels of their transfer because of a number of infirmities which emanate from the characteristics of the intangible assets. First, because of their 'public goods like' nature, the marginal cost of their use elsewhere is close to zero. Hence they are inefficiently priced (Magee 1977; Caves 1982: 5). Second, a severe information asymmetry exists which results from the inability of the seller to make a convincing *disclosure* about the intangible asset (Williamson 1981). This is particularly true in the case of unpatented process know-how. Third, the unaffiliated firms abroad may fail to recognize the productive potential of technological developments taking place in a country (Williamson 1981). Fourth, there may be *buyer's uncertainty* about the claims of the supplier regarding the potential value of the intangible asset (Caves 1982). Fifth, there may be problems with *codification* of knowledge. Certain kinds of knowledge may be embodied in the skills of personnel or may have a high 'tacit' component (Teece 1981, 1983). Finally, the arm's length market may fail to ensure uniform quality standards which are important, particularly in the case of the transfer of goodwill assets like brand names (Giddy and Rugman 1979).

These infirmities lead to a high cost of market transactions (transaction or governance costs) of intangible assets. Firms tend to avoid these costs by internalizing the transactions of the intangible assets. Firms that internalize transactions across national boundaries through FDI become multinational. Foreign investments under this theory, therefore, are a special case of horizontal expansion (Buckley and Casson 1976; Hennart 1982). Internalization eliminates transactions and hence transaction costs. However, there *are* certain costs associated with it. Co-ordination of manufacturing units located in geographical areas separated by national boundaries entails certain information costs. Further, the host country government may discriminate against enterprises under foreign control and hence there can be certain 'political' costs. In addition, there are administration costs of internal markets depending upon the degree of professionalization of management (Buckley and Casson 1976). Therefore, the economies arising from the internalization of transactions have to outweigh the costs associated with it; otherwise the transaction will take place through the external market. The net economies arising out of the elimination of transactions represent internalization incentives or advantages.

It must be pointed out that external markets for all intangible assets are not subject to the same degree of market failure, and hence costs involved in arm's length transactions also vary. Some of them can profitably be licensed at arm's length. For instance, the new proprietary 'process' technology as opposed to 'product' technology is more easily transferred at arm's length (Caves *et al.* 1980). For the process technologies that are standardized and can be 'written down and transmitted objectively, licensing may be a prime vehicle' (Caves 1974b). On the other hand, those process technologies that cannot be codified easily or embodied in capital goods because of a high tacit component are difficult to license (Teece 1981). Therefore, the 'propensities to internalize vary between industries' depending upon the costs of market transaction of intangible assets involved (Dunning 1981: 97).

In short, the recent propositions predict the incidence of FDI to be high in those branches of industry in which intangible assets characterized by locational and internalization incentives are important. The intangible assets approach (according to Hymer, Kindleberger, and Caves) predicts:

$$FS = FS\ (\underset{+}{OWN},\ \underset{+}{LOC}) \tag{3.1}$$

FS Share of foreign controlled enterprises in net industry sales—a proxy of incidence of FDI.

OWN A vector of proprietary intangible assets.

LOC A vector of locational advantages including the host government policy factors.

The signs (+, –) below the variables indicate the nature of relationships.

In the light of the transaction cost minimization theory, Function 3.1 can be modified as:

$$FS = FS\ (\underset{+}{OWN_i},\ \underset{+}{LOC}) \tag{3.2}$$

OWN_i A vector of intangible assets where market transfer entails high transaction costs, hence internalization advantages are present. OWN_i is a subset of OWN.

That is, the transfer of only those intangible assets which are characterized by high internalization incentives will take place through FDI. In the rest of the cases, arm's length licensing may be resorted to. It naturally follows that:

$$LCG = LCG\,(\underset{+}{OWN_n}, \underset{+}{LOC}) \tag{3.3}$$

LCG Incidence of arm's length licensing of intangible assets.

OWN_n A vector of intangible assets with relatively lower transaction costs and hence no internalization incentives. OWN_n is a subset of OWN.

An attempt towards verification of these postulates necessitates (*a*) the classification of the elements of vector OWN between OWN_i and OWN_n depending upon the transaction costs involved in their potential market transfer, and (*b*) the identification of variables that can proxy the significance of different elements of vectors OWN and LOC for the industry. While for the latter one can draw from the existing studies, the former is a more complex task as it is subject to qualitative judgements. In what follows, the nature of market failures that may be involved in potential market transfer of different intangible assets is assessed in order to classify them in OWN_i and OWN_n. The variables proxying the significance of these intangible assets for the industry normally used in the literature will also be indicated.

Classification of Intangible Assets

Product Differentiation and Goodwill

The goodwill associated with a firm's brand names or trade marks in the form of consumer loyalty is considered to be one of the most important intangible assets. In the case of brand or trade names, strict quality control is of critical importance. If rights to use brand or trade names are transferred to unassociated parties abroad, the firm runs the risk of dissipation of goodwill if the licensees fail to maintain the quality standards of the original producer (Giddy and Rugman 1979). Hence, transaction costs tend to be high because of the need to supervise quality. Another characteristic feature concerns the existence of other market failures, such as buyers' uncertainty due to lack of knowledge of the brand name's potential revenue productivity with the prospective licensee (Caves 1982, ch. 1). These factors result in a high cost of market transfer, making it a less efficient mode of transfer of goodwill assets for the owning firm.

Differentiation of a product through brand names usually involves advertising to communicate its differential features to potential buyers. Hence inter-industry variation in the intensity of advertising expenditures has been used in the literature as a proxy for the extent of product differentiation or the significance of the goodwill (Caves 1974a). Advertising intensity (ADS) will be used as a proxy for this intangible asset in our analysis as well.

ADS Advertising expenditure as a proportion of net sales, averaged over three years: 1978–79 to 1980–81 (for data sources and methodology, see Appendix I).

Knowledge:

Possession of knowledge, be it in the form of new technology or superior organizational or marketing skills, is also considered a valued intangible asset. Market transactions of different kinds of knowledge are subject to market failures of different intensities, as observed earlier. Two types of knowledge will be distinguished here in view of the availability of proxies: knowledge embodied in employee skills, and knowledge embodied in capital goods.

Market transfer of idiosyncratic knowledge is subject to high transaction costs because it necessitates physical transfer of personnel. Therefore, internalization incentives may be high in activities that depend more on learned or tacit skills (Williamson 1981; Teece 1981, 1983). Measurement of the industry's requirement of idiosyncratic knowledge can be proxied by calculating the proportion of the total work force that are non-production workers ($SKIL_1$). Non-production workers include supervisory staff, and managerial, marketing, quality control, and research personnel (including those responsible for troubleshooting). Such measurement has also been used by, among others, Caves (1974a), and Lall and Siddharthan (1982), to capture the industry's requirement of organizational and managerial skills. $SKIL_1$ will be used as a proxy for the industry's requirement of tacit knowledge.

$SKIL_1$ Non-production workers as a proportion of the total work force in 1978–79.

As it is based on the numerical proportion of overhead personnel, $SKIL_1$ does not take note of qualitative differences or the level of sophistication of such personnel. Therefore, another variable which takes note of both quantitative and qualitative aspects of skill requirements, the earnings of high salaried employees as a proportion of the total wage and salaries bill ($SKIL_2$), will be used as an alternative proxy of skill intensity. It has also been employed by Siddharthan and Dasgupta (1983), and Lall and Mohammad (1983a), for similar purposes.

$SKIL_2$ Earnings of high salaried employees (those receiving Rs 3,000 per month or more) as a proportion of the total wages and salaries bill, averaged over three years: 1978–79 to 1980–81.

Market transfer of knowledge embodied in capital goods does not suffer from the market failures that the kind embodied in human skills does. The information asymmetry does not arise, because knowledge is embodied in the basic design of the capital goods. The potential buyer's uncertainties about the performance are usually taken care of by the guarantees rendered by the suppliers.[8] Therefore, the transaction costs do not seem to be high, which results in a weak incentive to internalize in the case of knowledge embodied in capital goods.

The intensity of the production process in capital goods (plant and machinery) can proxy the extent of knowledge embodied in them. Hence, the plant and machinery to sales ratio (PMS) will be employed to capture the intensity of industry in knowledge embodied in capital goods.

PMS Gross book value of plant and machinery to net sales ratio, in 1980–81.

Access to Sources of Capital

The access of MNEs to capital markets the world over is considered to be an important intangible asset. Therefore, they might enjoy an advantage in industries requiring heavy capital investments. Horst (1972b) and Bergsten *et al.* (1978) have found a positive relationship between capital requirements for establishing a plant of minimum economic size and the extent of outward FDI from the United States. The access to sources of capital, however, does not seem to be an intangible asset with high transaction costs as markets for portfolio investments are well developed. Internalization incentives, therefore, appear to be weak in this case in countries where capital markets are well developed.

The larger the volume of capital required for setting up a plant in an industry, the greater should be the attraction of the access to sources of capital. Hence, capital requirements for an average sized plant (in the absence of information on minimum economic scales) in the industry will be used as a proxy to this intangible asset (AKR).

AKR Total capital employed per firm in the industry, averaged over three years 1978–79 to 1980–81.

The four broad categories of intangible assets have, therefore, been classified on the basis of expected transaction costs involved in potential market transfers in the subsets OWN_i and OWN_n of vector OWN as summarized in Table 3.1.

Table 3.1

Classification of Intangible Assets According to Transaction Costs

	Intangible asset	*Measurement*	*Transaction cost*	*Sub-vector*
1.	Product differentiation (goodwill)	ADS	high	OWN_i
2.	Knowledge			
	(*a*) embodied in human skills	$SKIL_1$	high	OWN_i
		$SKIL_2$	high	OWN_i
	(*b*) embodied in capital goods	PMS	low	OWN_n
3.	Access to sources of capital	AKR	low	OWN_n

Locational Advantages

In what follows, the factors that give rise to locational advantages and the variables proxying them will be identified. These advantages determine whether intangible assets are to be exploited in the home country or abroad; they do not determine the mode of foreign operations. Among these may be various components of the host government's policy, which make imports costly or difficult or subsidize local production, the communication/transportation costs, and inter-country differences in factor prices and productivity. Since we deal here with the variation in the incidence of FDI and licensing across different industries within a country, the inter-country differences in factor prices, transport costs, etc., are not important. For our purpose, therefore, elements of the government's trade and industrial policies are the relevant locational factors.

Foremost among the government policy factors relevant for local production in India are the import substitution programmes and protection accorded to local manufacturing. Ever since Independence, the Government of India has pursued a vigorous programme of industrialization based on import substitution within a framework of development planning. Heavy emphasis placed on import substitution persuaded the erstwhile foreign suppliers to undertake local manufacturing. Local manufacturing was also subsidized by the government through a host of incentives, cheap credit, infrastructural facilities, and the like. These factors, not only made local production more attractive than exports to India, but sometimes it even became a necessity for an MNE to keep its market in India intact. In a survey of British firms operating in India, Davies (1977) found import restrictions to have brought about local production in an overwhelming number of cases.

Although import substitution and protection have enjoyed an outstanding place in public policy framework in India, their direct measurement at the industry level poses a problem. Since the coverage of the Indian import substitution programme extended to almost everything that was not produced in the country, imports as a proportion of total supplies in the early phase of industrialization could be a reasonable proxy for the coverage of import substitution (ISP).

ISP Imports to local production ratio in 1960–61.

The degree of protection accorded to an industry is usually measured in terms of the effective rates of protection (ERPs). ERPs, however, have been changing over the years depending upon the intensity of local requirements and production (Panchamukhi 1977). This fact should be borne in mind while interpreting the relationship between ERPs in any particular year and the intensity of *cumulative* FDI or licensing. We shall use the NCAER (National Council of Applied Economic Research) series of estimates of ERP as a measure of protection.

ERP Effective rates of protection for the year 1979–80, Cordon method.

Government policy since Independence has sought to restrict foreign collaboration in areas where local skills were available. Such industries were mainly consumer goods industries incorporating relatively simple technology. Therefore, government policy is expected to have discouraged foreign collaboration in these industries. To capture the possible influence of this policy we shall distinguish consumer goods industries by using a dummy variable DCON.

DCON A dummy variable taking a value of one if the industry is producing consumer goods and zero otherwise.

Another component of public policy relevant for the industrial distribution of FDI and licensing is the industrial policy of the government. Through its industrial policy the government intends to direct the flow of investible resources (particularly since 1973) of foreign companies and large Indian firms (covered under the Monopolies and Restrictive Trade Practices Act 1969) to a set of priority or 'core' industries (Government of India, Ministry of Industry 1982). In the case of foreign companies, however, this policy has two drawbacks. First, foreign companies for the purposes of enforcement of this policy are those having over 40 per cent foreign ownership. But as observed in chapter 1, most of the FCEs have diluted their foreign equity to 40 per cent as per FERA directives (barring some exceptions). Second, it is applicable only to the further expansion of existing companies and to those entering after 1973. Thus, the scope of this policy is limited. It may still be interesting to examine its influence in attracting investible resources belonging to both FCEs and other large companies to the specified core industries. These industries will be identified with the help of the dummy variable DCORE.

DCORE A dummy variable taking a value of one if the industry was included in Appendix I of 'Industrial Policy—Government Decisions' 1973, and zero otherwise.

Having identified the elements of vectors OWN_i, OWN_n and LOC, we can now formulate the hypotheses. By substituting the specific elements of vector OWN_i and LOC in Equation 3.2 one would expect FS to be significantly and positively related to ADS, $SKIL_1/SKIL_2$, ISP, ERP, DCORE, and inversely to DCON. One would not expect the elements of vector OWN_n, i.e., PMS and AKR, to be important in determining FS if the postulates of the transaction cost minimization theory are correct. Similarly, elements of OWN_n and LOC, namely, PMS, AKR, ISP, ERP, DCON, and DCORE alone (and not of OWN_i, i.e., ADS, $SKIL_1/SKIL_2$) are expected to be important in explaining variation in LCG.

Most studies explaining inter-industry variation in foreign share in Canada have used R&D intensity of the industry in the United States to capture the innovativeness or technological intensity of the industry; usually they have found a positive relationship. Such a proxy cannot be used in India's case because no specific country has been the source of the bulk of FDI. We have data on R&D intensity of Indian industry. However, if the country depends for most innovations on foreign sources, as do most developing countries including India, the local R&D intensity may not reflect the innovativeness or technological intensity of the industry. On the other hand, the amount spent on R&D in the host country, which is usually of an adaptive nature, might reflect the level of domestic technological capabilities in adapting/absorbing technology if not really in generating it. If that, indeed, is the case then foreign collaborations, particularly FDIs, may be excluded from such industries because the selective policy of the Government of India does not normally allow foreign collaboration in industries where certain local technological capabilities have been built up. Therefore, the usual prediction applicable to technological intensity will not be valid in the case of local R&D intensity. None the less, it would be interesting to examine the relationship between local R&D intensity (RDS) and foreign collaboration (FS and LCG).

RDS Reported in-house R&D expenditure as a proportion of sales, averaged over three years: 1978–79 to 1980–81.

Thus the final equations to be estimated are:

$$FS = FS\ (ADS,\ SKIL_1,\ SKIL_2,\ PMS,\ AKR,\ ISP,\ ERP,\ DCON,\ DCORE,\ RDS) \qquad (3.4)$$

where coefficients of ADS, $SKIL_1$, $SKIL_2$, ISP, ERP, and DCORE are all expected to be positive and significantly different from zero; that of DCON is to be negative; and those of PMS and AKR are expected to be not significantly different from zero. No predictions are possible regarding the sign and significance of the coefficient of RDS. Similarly,

$$LCG = LCG\ (PMS,\ AKR,\ ADS,\ SKIL_1,\ SKIL_2,\ ISP,\ ERP,\ DCON,\ DCORE,\ RDS) \qquad (3.5)$$

where coefficients of PMS, AKR, ISP, ERP, and DCORE are expected to be positive and significantly different from zero; that of DCON is to be negative and significant; those of ADS, $SKIL_1$, and $SKIL_2$ are not likely to be significantly different from zero; and the sign and significance of coefficient of RDS is uncertain.

The measurements of FS and LCG are as follows:

FS Share of foreign controlled companies (with 25 per cent or more foreign equity) in net sales of all companies included in the data source in an industry, averaged over three years: 1978–79 to 1980–81.

The extent of licensing is proxied through the relative significance of payments for import of technology and other intangible assets, such as brand names and patents, and is defined as:

LCG Total royalty, technical, or other professional fees paid abroad as a proportion of net industry sales, averaged over three years: 1978–79 to 1980–81.

Caution needs to be applied while interpreting the results as there may be some overlapping in FS and LCG. Sometimes companies with FDI also remit royalty or technical fees. Second, unlike FDI, the technical and licensing agreements are of a limited duration (5 to 7 years). Hence, while FS reflects cumulative position, LCG relates to current licensing contracts.

Empirical Analysis

The hypotheses put forward above are tested by fitting Equations 3.4 and 3.5 with data for 49 three-digit Indian manufacturing industries (variable set I, see Appendix I for details).[9] The dependent variables in both the equations, FS and LCG, are non-negative ratios. When fitted in their original form, their predicted values for some observations were found to be negative. Logarithmic transformation was used, therefore, to prevent the predicted values from becoming negative.[10] All the independent variables, except dummy variables, were also expressed in logarithms, which necessitated adding small positive values to the observations having zero values. The logarithmic transformation of all the variables also helps to reduce any possible heteroscedasticity.[11]

The correlation matrix is given in Table 3.2. The correlation between FS and LCG is insignificant ($r = 0.0797$), thus, assuring the independence of FDI from licensing. Buckley and Davies (1981) have also reported similar independence between the relative significance of FDI and licensing in foreign production by British firms. The alternative measurements of idiosyncratic knowledge, $SKIL_1$ and $SKIL_2$, are highly correlated ($r = 0.698$), as expected. Several other independent variables are also found to be correlated. The proxies of knowledge embodied in capital goods (PMS) and capital requirements (AKR) are significantly correlated with each other. The relationship between policy variables and structural variables may throw some light on the nature of public policies in India. For instance, ISP is significantly related with $SKIL_1$, $SKIL_2$, DCORE with a positive sign, and DCON with a negative sign. This implies that the potential of import substitution existed in skill intensive branches of manufacturing, and those producing capital or intermediate goods. Such branches of manufacturing have also enjoyed high priority under the industrial policy. DCORE is also significantly related to $SKIL_2$, PMS, and AKR—which implies that priority sector industries are intensive in capital requirements and in knowledge of both kinds: idiosyncratic knowledge and that embodied in capital goods. ERP is correlated with ADS, which implies that relatively higher tariffs have been imposed on finished goods that are usually sold under brand names coupled with advertising.

Table 3.2
Correlation Matrix

(Log x Log)

	FS	LCG	ADS	$SKIL_2$	$SKIL_1$	PMS	AKR	RDS	ISP	ERP	DCORE	DCON
FS	1.000											
LCG	.079	1.000										
ADS	.176	-.127	1.000									
$SKIL_2$	.520	.293	.104	1.000								
$SKIL_1$	.445	.244	.085	.697	1.000							
PMS	.108	.455	-.372	.078	-.017	1.000						
AKR	.207	.304	-.246	.286	.192	.447	1.000					
RDS	-.197	.526	.018	.146	.204	.178	.052	1.000				
ISP	.582	.290	.083	.467	.507	.150	.078	.015	1.000			
ERP	.138	-.080	.367	-.145	-.198	.087	.192	.041	-.132	1.000		
DCORE	.277	.679	-.272	.389	.284	.324	.327	.249	.388	-.233	1.000	
DCON	-.208	-.540	.419	-.092	-.164	-.347	-.205	-.256	-.353	.266	-.572	1.000

The regression results for the two dependent variables are presented in Table 3.3. Because of multicollinearity between alternative measurements of the same variable and between some other variables, a few alternative combinations were tried. The fitted regressions are significant at the one per cent level in terms of F-statistics, and the industry characteristics identified here are able to explain over half (nearly two-thirds if all the explanatory variables are included) of the variation in the intensities of FS and LCG. The performance of individual explanatory variables in these equations is discussed below.

Table 3.3
Regression Equations Explaining Variation in Intensity of FDI and Licensing in Indian Manufacturing

Dependent variable			*FS*			*LCG*
Explanatory variable	*(i)*	*(ii)*	*(iii)*	*(iv)*	*(i)*	*(ii)*
1. ADS	0.348[b]	0.278[c]	0.295[b]	0,271	0.170	0.262
	(2.426)	(1.917)	(2.006)	(1.667)	(0.934)	(1.276)
2. $SKIL_2$	2.267[a]	2.441[a]				0.102
	(4.062)	(4.618)				(0.125)
3. $SKIL_1$			1.517[c]	3.041[a]	–0.444	
			(1.743)	(3.665)	(–0.412)	
4. PMS		–0.466				1.199[b]
		(–1.069)				(2.031)
5. AKR	0.202		0.352	0.183	0,409	0.109
	(0.739)		(1.298)	(0.611)	(1.218)	(0.285)
6. RDS	–0.313[a]	–0.299[a]	–0.273[b]	–0.325[a]	0.438[a]	0.385[a]
	(–3.210)	(–3.064)	(–2.694)	(–3.207)	(3.485)	(3.148)
7. ISP			0.310[b]		0.055	–0.016
			(2.367)		(0.341)	(0.102)
8. ERP				0.799		0.004
				(1.517)		(0.007)
9. DCORE			0.355		2.699[a]	2.633[a]
			(0.590)		(3.679)	(3.523)
10. DCON	–1.575[a]	–1.703[a]	–0.678	–1.575[a]	–1.189	–1.122
	(–2.886)	(–3.105)	(–1.047)	(–2.747)	(–1.484)	(–1.395)
Constant	–7.980[a]	–7.368[a]	–10.645[a]	–16.586[a]	–4.947	–2.834
	(–3.835)	(–5.325)	(–3.476)	(–4.332)	(–1.304)	(–0.738)
$\bar{R}^2$	0.475	0.482	0.504	0.451	0.634	0.669
F	7.78[a]	8.01[a]	5.96[a]	5.75[a]	10.17[a]	8.79[a]
d.f.	43	43	41	42	41	39

Note: Figures in parentheses are t-values. Superscripts indicate levels of significance (two-tailed tests) as follows: a=99%, b=95%, and c=90%.

Intangible Assets

The product differentiation variable ADS has a positive sign and is statistically significant in all the equations that explain variation in FS, except in equation (*iv*) in Table 3.3. The inclusion of ERP in equation (*iv*) adversely affects the level of significance of ADS because of their mutual correlation; ADS is not significant in any equation that explains variation in LCG. These findings are in tune with the theoretical predictions and, therefore, uphold the hypothesis that market transfers of goodwill assets are subject to high transaction costs due to buyers' uncertainty, and quality supervision costs. Hence, markets for such intangible assets tend to be internalized through FDI.

The variables used as proxies for idiosyncratic knowledge, $SKIL_1$ and $SKIL_2$ are both significant, with positive signs in the equations that explain FS. The inclusion of ISP, which is correlated with both $SKIL_1$ and $SKIL_2$, affects the level of their significance adversely (as in equation (*iii*)). On the other hand, none of the human skill variables is significant at all in explaining variation in LCG. This finding again supports our hypothesis. Licensing seems to be an inefficient channel of transfer of knowledge when it is embodied in the skills of personnel; hence FDI is resorted to.

The variable used as a proxy for knowledge embodied in capital goods, PMS, has a negative sign and is not significantly different from zero in the FS equations. In the equations explaining LCG, however, it turns out to be significant with a positive sign. This finding indicates, as per the hypothesis, that the cost of external market transactions is not too high (when knowledge is embodied in capital goods) to make it an inefficient mode of transfer. Licensing and not FDI is, therefore, a preferred mode in such cases.

The variable capturing the ownership advantage of access to sources of capital, AKR, is not significant in any equation explaining either FS or LCG. The unimportance of AKR in both the cases suggests that access to sources of capital is no longer a source of monopolistic advantage for MNEs in India. This may be due to the development of capital markets and the emergence of government-sponsored industrial development banks and financial institutions in the country.

The variable used as a proxy for R&D intensity, RDS, is significant in both sets of equations, but with different signs. In the case of FS it has a negative sign whereas it turns out with a positive sign in LCG equations. This finding can be explained in terms of available evidence on the nature of in-house R&D in India. Desai (1980) has found that the R&D activity of Indian firms normally consists of minor adaptations to imported technology made to suit local tastes, market size, and raw materials. Further, Katrak (1985) concludes from his study of R&D in India that the propensity to adapt imported technologies decreases with its complexity. Hence the proportion of local R&D spending may be inversely related to the complexity of technology. More complex technologies may be difficult to transfer through external markets because of limitations in the absorptive capacity of developing country firms, apart from other market failures. Hence, they may be transferred through the package of FDI. That is how there might exist an inverse relationship between FS and RDS, and a positive association between LCG and RDS. However, more detailed work on the nature and characteristics of in-house R&D activity in India and its relationship with technology transfers is needed before a more definitive statement on this relationship can be made.

Locational Advantages

The coefficient of ISP is positive and significant in explaining variations in FS. The effective protection variable (ERP) has a positive sign and is significant only at the 15 per cent level in the FS equation. However, neither of these variables is significant in explaining variations in LCG. While performance of ISP in the FS equation is as per the hypothesis, its insignificance in LCG's case may be attributable to differences in measurements of FS and LCG. As pointed out earlier, unlike FS, LCG relates to a more recent period. The import substitution potential which existed in the late 1950s cannot be expected to be related to foreign technical collaborations approved during the last 5 to 7 years. Apart from limitations of measurement in adequately reflecting the changing levels of protection over the years, ERPs have been found to be insignificant in most of the studies explaining FS in Canada (Caves 1974a; Caves *et al.* 1980; Owen 1982; Gupta 1983).

Of the other policy variables, the consumer goods dummy

variable DCON has a negative sign throughout in both FS and LCG equations, and is significant in the absence of ISP with which is it collinear. The performance of DCON is, therefore, as per expectation. The selective policy towards foreign collaborations (both FDI and licensing) which the government has followed throughout the post-Independence period seems to have discouraged FCEs in consumer goods sectors where local skills have been available. The other policy variable which captures the effect of industrial policies, DCORE, has a positive sign in both sets of equations but is significant only in explaining LCG. One reason for its failure to explain FS may be that this policy is applicable only to the further expansion of FCEs with more than 40 per cent foreign equity. Such companies constitute only a part of those defined to be FCEs here. Furthermore, the policy evolved only during the 1970s and hence could not have influenced, in any significant manner, the industrial pattern of cumulative FDI, which FS reflects.

The above findings show that the theoretical predictions emanating from recent propositions in the theory of international operations of the firm are able to explain inter-industry differences in intensities of FDI and licensing in Indian manufacturing fairly well. FDI has been found to be a dominant mode of operation in industries characterized by a high level of product differentiation and with high skill requirements. In contrast, industries which are intensive in the use of capital goods for production, and require less complex technologies, are dominated by licensing. Access to sources of capital no longer seems to provide an edge to an MNE in the Indian market.

Conclusions

This chapter has analysed the determinants of variations in the share of FCEs in sales across 49 manufacturing industries in India. At the outset an attempt was made to formulate hypotheses on the basis of recent theories of the internationalization of firms, particularly the transaction cost minimization paradigm. The theory suggests that FDI will take place only when market transfer of intangible assets involves high transaction costs. In the rest of the cases the transfer will take place through arm's length licensing. To have a fuller verification of the predictions of the theory, parallel analyses of the determinants of the intensity of FDI and licensing were made for the same set of industries.

The empirical results obtained for Indian industries suggest, in line with the hypotheses, that FDI has concentrated in those branches of manufacturing which are characterized by a high degree of product differentiation and in branches that are intensive in the use of idiosyncratic knowledge. Licensing seems to be a dominant mode in industries which are intensive in the use of knowledge embodied in capital goods. The access to sources of capital is not important for both FDI and licensing, and seems to have lost its importance as an intangible asset capable of giving an edge to MNEs in the Indian market. This may be due to the development of capital markets and the emergence of a number of government sponsored financial institutions in India.

The R&D intensity of local industry is found to be inversely related to the intensity of FDI but positively related to that of licensing. This finding has been interpreted in the light of the earlier evidence that local in-house R&D in India is usually of an adaptive nature and that the tendency to adapt decreases with the complexity of technology. As more complex technologies may be difficult to transfer through licensing, FDI could be the preferred mode of transfer.

FDI is also found to have concentrated in import-competing sectors. Hence the import substitution programme of the government seems to have encouraged the erstwhile exporters to the country to set up local production facilities. The selective policy which the government has followed appears to have discouraged foreign collaborations of either kind in consumer goods industries where local skills are available in some measure. The government's industrial policy, which attaches priority to certain industries with high linkages, seems to have attracted considerable investment and technology to those sectors.

The choice between FDI and licensing can sometimes be influenced by the intervention of the host government at the time of entry. The Indian government has periodically issued lists of items for which foreign technical collaborations (licensing) and foreign financial collaborations (FDI) could be permitted. Certain firm- and technology-specific factors also play a role in influencing the choice of the mode of foreign participation, such as age, size, past experience in technology transfer, extent of product and geographical diversification of the firm, the degree of sophistication of the technological advance, etc. (Telesio 1979; Davidson and McFetridge 1984). Given the level of industrial aggregation these factors could not, however, be captured in the present exercise.

Notes

1. Horst (1972b), Baldwin (1979), Bergsten *et al.* (1978), Pugel (1978, 1981), Lall (1980a) and Swedenborg (1979) have used a similar framework to explain inter-industry variation in outward FDI from the home countries: the United States in all the cases except the last which is for Swedish FDI.
2. Licensing in this study refers to all those contractual agreements between business firms of two countries involving transfer of some intangible asset, such as right to use brand name or patent, the transfer of technology, or turn-key plant construction in which the licensor does not hold the controlling interest.
3. Dunning (1984), Davidson and McFetridge (1984, 1985), and Contractor (1984) have undertaken the verification of these propositions in inter-country studies.
4. We shall concentrate here only on horizontal foreign expansion because in India's case the bulk of foreign investments in the manufacturing sector are of this type.
5. Horst (1972a), Hirsch (1976), Baldwin (1979), Lall (1980a), and Buckley and Pearce (1981) have found evidence on interdependence of exports and FDI.
6. Buckley and Davies (1981) provide evidence on licensing fast gaining significance as a mode of foreign production by British firms in the 1970s. For evidence on increasing replacement of FDI by licensing see Oman (1984).
7. Different versions of these propositions exist, for example, eclectic or OLI (ownership, locational and internalization) theory (Dunning), internalization (Rugman), transaction cost minimization (Williamson, Teece), appropriability (Magee), and transactional approach (Caves).
8. In the case of developing country firms that have recently emerged as technology suppliers, however, the buyer's uncertainty may persist despite guarantees because of the lack of an established reputation. Hence, markets are often internalized (Wells 1983). This is usually not the case with advanced country investors with whom we deal here.
9. The original variable set had 54 branches of manufacturing industry. Five of them, however, were left out of the empirical analysis: safety matches, tobacco products (not elsewhere specified), iron and steel, and two miscellaneous industries.

10. In addition to logarithmic transformation, logistic transformation of the type log (FS/I-FS) was also tried The OLS results for the two transformations were not very much different. Since logit transformation makes interpretation of relationships difficult, we report results pertaining to logarithmic transformation only.
11. See Maddala (1979, ch. 12).

4

Discriminating Characteristics of Foreign and Local Enterprises in Indian Manufacturing

Introduction

Studies evaluating the impact of FDI on host developing countries have usually addressed themselves to quantifying gross or net generation of incomes, savings, foreign exchange, and employment by individual or total FDI projects [Bos *et al.* (1974); Lall and Streeten (1977); Weiss (1980); Kumar (1980, 1984); Pursell (1981); ILO (1981); and Rugman (1980a)]. This evaluation approach ignores the domestic alternative that may be possible in most cases (with or without foreign technology and loans). The direct balance of payment (BOP) effect in the case of an import substitution project is very likely to be negative and could be so even in the case of a local firm. From the point of view of evaluating the impact of FCEs on various parameters of development, therefore, examination of aspects that distinguish them from their local counterparts is more important. Furthermore, it has been argued, for instance by Cohen (1975), and Newfarmer and Marsh (1981), that the impact of FDI on development would be 'minimal' if foreign controlled and local firms behaved in a similar way.

The current state of knowledge on conduct and performance differences between foreign and local firms in developing countries is deficient in many respects. Besides having a small sample size and a limited choice of parameters, the existing studies have seldom controlled for extraneous influences and interaction among the variables, since most of them have been conducted using univariate analysis (see Lall 1981, ch. 2; Caves 1982, ch. 9, for surveys).

This chapter compares some important aspects of conduct and performance of foreign controlled and local firms (FCEs and LCEs respectively) in 49 Indian manufacturing industries[1] in a more comprehensive framework. The analysis covers different elements of market structure and performance, choice of technology, employee compensation behaviour, linkages with the domestic economy, export performance, and financial policy and management. The significance of the differences between the two groups of firms across 49 industries is first evaluated in terms of a univariate statistical criterion (Wilcoxon's Signed Ranks Test). The variables identified by the univariate test as important in differentiating between the two groups are then simultaneously included in a multivariate test to control for possible mutual interaction. The final discriminating variables are, thus, selected through step-wise discriminant analysis from among those identified by the univariate analysis.

First, the characteristics of MNEs which may lead to differences in the behaviour of FCEs and LCEs are examined. In the light of these characteristics and the existing empirical evidence, a set of hypotheses on the expected nature of differences pertaining to different parameters are formulated. The findings of the empirical analysis in the univariate and multivariate frameworks, respectively, are presented. The chapter concludes with a summary of the major findings and the limitations of the analysis.

Differences Between FCEs and LCEs—Hypotheses

FCEs share the ownership of certain unique intangible assets with parent MNEs, such as brand goodwill, knowledge, organizational skills, access to marketing and information networks, etc. These ownership advantages make the asset bundles of FCEs different from those of their local counterparts. This fact may lead to differences in the mode of rivalry between the two groups of firms. The FCEs' rivalry may be dominated by non- price competition based on product differentiation to maximize the revenue productivity of advantages, such as the brand goodwill, that they hold (Caves 1974b). The mode of rivalry might reflect on their scale of operations, advertising behaviour, and profit margins. The access to information on world markets and opportunities coupled with the MNEs' objective of global profit maximization may result in rationalization of production on the basis of international division of labour, which may lead to a higher dependence of FCEs on international trade. FCEs' perception of risks may also be different because of their access to better information. The centralization of strategic decision-making responding to global opportunities in MNEs may lead to a different investment and financing behaviour, propensity to undertake R&D, raw material sourcing, export behaviour, profit repatriation behaviour, etc., of FCEs (Newfarmer and Marsh 1981). The decisions to enter, diversify, and undertake R&D of MNE affiliates in Canada have been found to be determined less by local conditions than in the case of their local counterparts (Gorecki 1976, 1980; Howe and McFetridge 1976). The factor proportions and employee compensation behaviour may show differences because of the grooming of MNEs in an environment of capital abundance or labour scarcity. The experienced and more professional organizational skills of MNEs may lead to more optimal financial and inventory management.

Taking into account these general characteristics of MNEs, and drawing upon existing empirical knowledge, we have formulated hypotheses concerning the nature of the differences between FCEs and their local counterparts in terms of different parameters of behaviour. These parameters have been classified into seven broad headings: market structure, conduct, and performance; choice of technique; employee compensation behaviour; vertical inter-firm linkage generation in the local economy; export performance; financial policy and tax planning; and financial management. The variables used as proxies for each of these parameters and their definitions are also indicated.

Market Structure, Conduct, and Performance

The direct and indirect (through their competitive behaviour) impact of the penetration of MNEs on host country market structures has received considerable attention in the recent literature. Market structure and performance can be influenced by FCEs through the relative scale of their operation, and other aspects of competitive behaviour. In some countries, particularly in Latin America, there is evidence that MNEs have influenced local market structures through their acquisition and merger behaviour (Evans 1979). These, however, are not important in the Indian case because of government regulations.

Scale of Operations

The scale of operation of firms is an important determinant of the market structure of the industry. There are no clear-cut *a priori* reasons for expecting differences in the relative scales of operations of FCEs and their local counterparts. However, as has been observed earlier, FCEs are expected to prefer non-price competition and sell more differentiated products. Such form of rivalry is often accompanied by extensive advertising and marketing campaigns to disseminate the differentiating features of the product among potential customers. The advertising activity enjoys significant economies of scale and is most cost effective if carried out at the national scale rather than at regional or local levels (Comanor and Wilson 1974). It can, therefore, be expected that FCEs will prefer to set up operations that intend to serve national markets. Hence, the relative scale of their operations is likely to be larger than that of a firm not following a similar strategy. This expectation perhaps explains the conclusion by Lall (1981, ch. 2: 43), reached on the basis of a survey, that the 'larger and more industrially advanced a host economy, the more will TNC affiliates tend to exceed their local competitors in size'.

That FCEs are on average larger than their local counterparts is indicated by the available empirical evidence provided, for example, by Kidron (1965: 224) in the case of India; Newfarmer and Mueller (1975) for Mexico and Brazil; and Lall and Streeten (1977, ch. 6) for India, Colombia and Malaysia.

A number of studies have observed a significant correlation between the degree of presence of MNEs and seller concentration. Examples are: Rosenbluth (1970) in the case of Canada; Radhu (1973) for Pakistan; Willmore (1976) for Guatemala; Newfarmer and Mueller (1975) and Connor (1977) for Mexico and Brazil; and Parry (1980) for Australia. These correlations, however, can be misleading, as the sources of entry barriers that give rise to concentration and the sources of FDI overlap substantially (Caves 1982). Evans (1977) for Brazil, Lall (1979) for Malaysia, and Blomstrom (1986) for Mexico find the positive influence of foreign ownership on industry concentration even after controlling for the entry barriers.

In view of the theoretical reasoning, and in the light of the empirical evidence, the scale of operations of FCEs will be hypothesized to be larger than that of their local counterparts in Indian manufacturing. The scale of operation will be proxied through the average volume of net sales per firm ($SIZE_i$).

$SIZE_i$ Average net sales per firm in the ith group (i = FCE, LCE throughout).

Conduct

Firms manipulate the external constraints placed on their expansion through their advertising, R&D, product diversification, collusion, merger and takeover behaviour (Hay and Morris 1979: 30). In view of the limitations of data on product diversification and collusion behaviour, and government regulations on merger and takeovers, we shall consider only the advertising and R&D.

Advertising: Advertising activity is the source of brand goodwill and an important aspect of non-price rivalry. However, there is a general lack of evidence on the comparative advertising behaviour of FCEs and local firms. Caves (1974b: 22) has argued that the skill of MNEs in differentiating their products prompt them to prefer non-price competitive rivalry, such as through advertising campaigns. The presence of MNEs may dispose an industry towards non-price competition and hence, may increase the general level of advertising expenditure of the industry (Dunning 1981, ch. 7). Caves *et al*. (1980), and Gupta (1983), found the foreign share in industry sales to have a significant positive influence in explaining the proportion of advertising expenditure in Canadian manufacturing industries. This could be due to two reasons: one, the foreign subsidiaries spend a relatively higher proportion to their income on advertising so that the industry average of advertising expenditure rises in proportion to their presence; and two, the foreign subsidiaries induce the industry to pursue non-price rivalry, and both foreign and local firms spend a higher proportion of income on advertising. Which of the two effects is dominant, however, is not clear from the two studies. Willmore (1986) found FCEs to spend a higher proportion of sales revenue on advertising than their local counterparts in Brazil even after controlling for firm size and industry. We shall, therefore, examine the hypothesis that FCEs spend a higher proportion of their income on advertising (ADS_i) than their local counterparts.

ADS_i Advertising expenditures of ith group of firms as a proportion of net industry sales in 1980–81.

Research and development: R&D activity is the main source of the technological edge that MNEs enjoy. It is logical, therefore, to expect MNEs to concentrate their R&D activity near their headquarters (Vernon 1974). The US Tariff Commission (1973) confirmed that US MNEs do concentrate most of their R&D in the United States. Creamer (1976), on the basis of a survey of over 900 US MNEs having overseas R&D, found that the bulk of their R&D activity was undertaken in the United States only. A similar trend was reported by Mansfield *et al.* (1979) in a more recent survey. Furthermore, the overseas R&D was carried out primarily in the industrialized countries (two-thirds of the total overseas R&D activity done by US MNEs being in three countries, namely, Canada, the United Kingdom, and West Germany). Only a 'negligible share' of the overseas R&D found its way to the developing countries. The implication of this finding is that affiliates of MNEs, particularly in the developing countries, are likely to undertake little R&D.

On the other hand, there may be several compelling reasons for a local firm to undertake R&D. For instance, local firms do not enjoy continuous access to laboratories of the parent firm abroad as FCEs do. The local firms that obtain technology from abroad on a licensing basis may be forced to undertake R&D to absorb, adapt, and modernize the technology. The fixed life span (usually 5 to 7 years) of foreign technical collaborations and restrictions placed by the Indian government on their renewal may make the licencees anxious to absorb the technology during the life of the collaboration agreement (Kumar 1987b).

Most of the studies that analysed R&D intensity found the locally controlled firms to be more R&D intensive than their foreign controlled counterparts. The examples are, Subrahmanian (1972) for the Indian chemical industry; UNCTAD (1983) for the Indian capital goods industry; Evans (1979), and Gordon and Fowler (1983) for the pharmaceutical industries in Brazil and Canada, respectively; and Ragachand (1981) in the case of Canada. On the basis of a detailed examination of different aspects of innovative activity of foreign and local firms in Latin American countries, controlling for age and scale of operation, Fairchild and Sosin (1986) reached the conclusion that domestic firms had a higher level of internal innovative activity, whereas foreign firms relied more heavily on sources external to the subsidiary. Lall (1985, ch. 7) found a positive relationship between foreign ownership and R&D in the Indian engineering industry but a negative one in the chemical industry, thus, affording no generalization. We shall verify the hypothesis that in India, FCEs spend a smaller proportion of their income on R&D (RDS_i) than their local counterparts.

RDS_i Reported in-house R&D expenditure of ith group of firms as a proportion of total sales in 1980–81.

Performance

The performance of FCEs and LCEs has been compared in terms of profitability and factor productivities. A number of studies have found higher labour productivity in the case of FCEs, for example, Fairchild and Sosin (1986) in various Latin American countries and Willmore (1986) in Brazil. But a large part of the difference could be on account of their observed higher capital intensity. Tyler (1978)in Brazil, Vendrell-Alda

(1978) in Argentina, and Agarwal (1979) in India, have attempted to compare total factor productivities of FCEs and LCEs. The differences appeared to be significant in the case of India. The lack of data on physical labour inputs, inflation adjusted book value of capital stock, physical quantity of output, and rates of capital utilization[2] (in our data base) does not permit us to make any meaningful comparison of performance in terms of factor productivities.[3] We shall, therefore, confine ourselves to comparisons of profitability and growth rate.

Profitability: FCEs are expected to enjoy higher profitability than their local counterparts because of their monopolistic ownership of intangible assets. It has been observed earlier that this may induce them to pursue a non-price mode of rivalry. A part of prices charged by them may be monopoly rents for goodwill and other intangible assets held. Evidence from the literature gives the impression that FCEs fare better than local firms in terms of profitability. However, when extraneous factors are controlled for, the observed differences do not remain statistically significant. The examples are, Lall (1976) for the case of Colombia and India; Gershenberg and Ryan (1978) for Uganda; and Fairchild and Sosin (1986) for the Latin American countries. Subrahmanian (1972), Fairchild (1977), and Newfarmer and Marsh (1981) also did not find any significant differences between profitability of FCEs and their local counterparts in Indian, Mexican, and Brazilian case studies, respectively.

The reported profits, however, need not necessarily reflect the true profits, since they are subject to possible manipulations such as transfer prices (Newfarmer and Marsh 1981; Lall 1981). We shall, none the less, examine whether FCEs have higher profitability. Following the current practice (Collins and Preston 1970; Hay and Morris 1979: 206), profit margins on sales (PCM_i) (Lerner's index) rather than the rate of return will be used to represent profitability.

PCM_i Profit before tax of ith group of firms as proportion of their net sales in 1980–81.

Growth: Growth is also an important aspect of the performance of firms. The managerial theories of the firm (Marris

1964) have considered maximization of growth to be the basic objective of the managerial firm (subject to a certain minimum profit constraint). The sources of growth may include expansion of the existing product line, vertical integration, conglomerate diversification, and acquisition. FCEs may be considered better equipped to undertake expansion, integration, or diversification for the reasons that facilitate their initial entry, namely, ownership advantages. However, the decision pertaining to the expansion of FCEs may be guided not only by local opportunities but also by the parent enterprise's global strategy. Furthermore, in India firms needed to procure an industrial licence from the government (and an additional clearance under the FERA or MRTP Acts for firms coming under their purview) before effecting any plans of substantial expansion of the existing product line, integration, diversification, or acquisition. Though the industrial policy statements of the government repeatedly assured all FCEs with foreign equity up to 40 per cent, a non-discriminatory treatment in industrial licensing, it is possible that the purely local firms enjoyed a preference over FCEs in the actual implementation of policy.

Thus, while FCEs may enjoy an edge over their local counterparts in terms of resources for growth, they may be constrained by the global strategy of the parent enterprise and Indian government policy. In the absence of information on the possible weights of these contradictory factors we are unable to reach a definite prediction on the relative rates of growth of FCEs and their counterparts. Empirical studies (for example, Siddharthan and Lall 1982; M.S. Kumar 1984) have usually confined themselves to comparisons of growth rates between developed country firms that stayed at home and those which undertook foreign investments and became multinational. Therefore, growth rates ($GROW_i$) of FCEs and local firms will be compared without *a priori* prediction.

$GROW_i$ Proportionate change in net sales of ith group of firms in industry over 1978–79 to 1980–81.

Choice of Technique

The choice of technique by foreign firms has perhaps been the most controversial issue till date. The *a priori* reasoning has been that technologies of FCEs are appropriate to the factor endowments of their home countries, which are typically capital abundant. Reuber *et al.* (1973, ch. 6) found that in over 70 per cent of the cases MNEs transferred process technology to developing countries without any adaptations. Courtney and Leipziger (1975), and Leipziger (1976), however, found that MNE subsidiaries in developing countries employed different techniques, in most cases more labour- intensive than their counterparts in industrialized countries. Among the several factors that might discourage adaptation of imported technology to make it more appropriate to the factor proportions of developing countries is the possibility of technological rigidity. Marsh *et al.* (1983) find a close association between capital intensity and technological rigidity. According to them MNEs usually concentrate in capital intensive sectors which often suffer from a technological rigidity that limits the scope for influencing technological choice. Morley and Smith (1977) reached similar conclusions.

Most studies that compare factor proportions have noted higher capital intensity of operations in foreign firms compared to local ones. The examples are, Forsyth and Solomon (1977) in the case of Ghana; Gershenberg and Ryan (1978) for Uganda; Newfarmer and Marsh (1981) for the Brazilian electrical equipment industry; Biersteker (1978) for Nigeria; Radhu (1973) for Pakistan; Wells (1973) for Indonesia; Agarwal (1976) for India; Jo (1980) for South Korea; Chen (1983) for Indonesia and Thailand; Balasubramanyam (1984) for Indonesia; Meller and Mizala (1982) for six Latin American countries; and Willmore (1986) in Brazil. On the other hand, Cohen (1975) in the case of Taiwan, South Korea and Singapore; Reidel (1975) for Taiwan, and Jo (1980) for South Korea found that export-oriented foreign subsidiaries did not employ a significantly different technology from that of the local export-oriented firms. Chung and Lee (1980) in the case of Korea; Mason (1973) in the case of Mexico and Philippines; and Chen (1983) in the case of Hong Kong, Malaysia, and Taiwan also could not find any significant difference in capital intensities, possibly due to the export-oriented nature of these economies. Kirim (1986) did not find any significant difference in capital intensity on the basis of nationality in the Turkish pharmaceutical industry (controlling for size and degree of vertical integration factors). ILO (1984), on the basis of studies in a number of developing countries noted that MNE affiliates tended to be more capital intensive but that their capital intensity was explained in terms of other characteristics, such as size rather than by multinationality.

The evidence, therefore, generally confirms the view that MNEs employ technology that is relatively more capital intensive compared to that used by local firms when producing mainly for local markets. In the case of manufacture for exports, however, FCEs employ technology not significantly different from that employed by their local counterparts. Since the firms studied here are predominantly local market-oriented we shall verify the higher capital intensity or, alternatively, lower labour intensity of FCEs as compared with their local counterparts. There are problems in measuring capital intensity due to the non-availability of data on the physical quantity of labour employed in company annual reports, our ultimate source of data. Measurement of capital also suffers from problems relating to different vintages of capital and rates of capital exhaustion (utilization), differing accounting rules, and price changes over time (Mason 1973). In the absence of any better index, we use a wages:fixed assets ratio as an admittedly crude indicator of the labour:capital ratio (LKR_i).

LKR_i Total wages and salaries bill of ith group of firms as a proportion of total fixed assets, in the year 1980–81.

Employee Compensation Behaviour/Qualitative Differences in Employee Skills

MNE affiliates are expected to pay higher wages and salaries than their local counterparts in developing countries because of their grooming in an environment of labour scarcity and high wages (Singer 1970). A number of studies seem to support this expectation, for instance, Markensten (1972) for Swedish MNEs in India; Gershenberg and Ryan (1978) for Uganda; Mason (1973) for the Philippines and, Mexico; Possas (1979) for Brazil; and ILO (1976). Chee (1980) reported that, while there was a significant difference between wage payments by foreign and local firms to managerial and skilled workers, no significant difference was observed in the case of unskilled workers (cited in Chen 1983: 147). Cohen (1975) did not find any clear pattern in the relative employee compensation behaviour of foreign firms in the case of export-oriented firms in South Korea, Singapore, and Taiwan. Lim (1977), while examining the determinants of average hourly wages in West Malaysian manufacturing industries, inferred that the higher wages paid by foreign firms were largely due to greater capital intensity and productivity of their production processes. Similar conclusions were reached by Dunning and Morgan (1980) in a six-country study where they observed that, normalizing for industry and country differences, MNEs do in general pay higher wages than indigenous firms but that the margin of difference is not as great as is sometimes alleged. Thus the existing evidence 'does not affirm any pervasive differences due strictly to their transnational status' (Caves 1982). Furthermore, a part of the higher wages paid by FCEs may be on account of possible differences in skills not controlled for in any of these studies. Balasubramanyam (1984) in the case of Indonesia, and Willmore (1986) in the case of Brazil find the average wages paid by FCEs to be significantly higher than their local counterparts, but they attribute them to differences in the quality of human capital. We shall, none the less, attempt to compare an index of employee compensation behaviour between foreign and local firms; expecting it to be higher for the former.

Measurement of the relative rates of wages and salaries, however, is not without problems. Companies in India do not generally report the total number of employees in their annual statements of accounts. Therefore, even though the total wage bill is presented, it is not possible to compute the average levels of wages. However, the number and the gross emoluments of all employees in receipt of Rs 3,000 per month or more are given. Siddharthan and Dasgupta (1983), and Lall and Mohammad (1983a) have used, as we did in the previous chapter, the proportion of earnings of high income employees in the total wage bill as a proxy of managerial and/or skill intensity

($SKIL_2$). The proportion of high income employees may differ between industries due to their differing skill requirements. However, one often finds wide variation in the proportion of such employees across different firms in the same industry. There could be two possible explanations for such intra-industry variation: (*a*) inter-firm variations in employee compensation behaviour or pay policies, or (*b*) inter-firm qualitative differences in skills (such as higher qualifications and experience or motivation). Hence, differences in the proportion of high income employees (HIE_i) between FCEs and LCEs may be due to variations in either pay policies or the quality of the personnel employed, or both. In both cases, FCEs are likely to have a higher HIE.

HIE_i Earnings of high income employees (those receiving Rs 3,000 per month or more) as a proportion of total salaries and wages bill of ith group of firms in 1980–81.

Vertical Inter-Firm Linkages with Domestic Economy

The vertical inter-firm linkages created by an enterprise have important implications for the development of the host economy. The volume of vertical backward linkages generated is determined by two decisions concerning the sourcing of raw materials and intermediate products of the firm: 'import or procure locally' and 'make or buy'. The performance of FCEs and LCEs will be compared in terms of both these aspects.

Importation versus Domestic Procurement

A number of studies have compared the dependence of foreign and local firms on imported raw materials in order to get an idea of the extent of linkages generated in the domestic economy. FCEs can be expected to import a higher proportion of their raw materials and other inputs than local firms, because of their familiarity with foreign suppliers and the alleged inadequacies of local producers (McAleese and McDonald 1978), and sometimes to provide a market for products of their associates elsewhere. Cohen (1975) in the case of South Korea, Taiwan, and Singapore, and Reidel (1975) in the case of Taiwan, have found that export-oriented foreign firms import a greater proportion of inputs than their local counterparts. Even foreign firms producing predominantly for domestic markets have been found to depend more on imports than their local counterparts, in studies by Kelkar (1977) and Subrahmanian and Pillai (1979) for India; McAleese and McDonald (1978) for Ireland; Jo (1980) for South Korea; and Newfarmer and Marsh (1981) for the Brazilian electrical industry. Lall and Streeten (1977), in a study of six countries including India, however, did not find any significant difference between the import dependence of foreign and local firms.

We shall verify the hypothesized higher dependence of FCEs on imported raw materials (IMP_i) for our sample of Indian manufacturing industries.

IMP_i Imported raw materials as a proportion of raw material consumption of ith group of firms in 1980–81.

To Make versus to Buy

The 'make or buy' decision essentially relates to the degree of vertical integration. The latter is inversely related to subcontracting parts of the production run to unassociated vendors. In countries like India, which have evolved a strict trade and exchange control regime that restricts the freedom of firms to import, subcontracting may be an important aspect of a firm's decision-making concerning the sourcing of intermediates and raw materials.

A number of market failures may tempt the firm to internalize the manufacture of intermediate inputs, such as the certainty of delivery schedules and quality standards (Williamson 1975; Jansson 1982). A certain monopoly rent may also be associated with vertical integration. On the other hand, firms can internalize part of the scale economies in the manufacture of intermediates and can escape problems of industrial relations by subcontracting their production to other firms. In India's case, promotion of subcontracting is also one of the objectives of the government's industrial policy (the promotion of ancillary industries). The degree of vertical integration will, therefore, be determined by the relative weights of these factors which may vary from industry to industry and from firm to firm. There are no clues as to whether FCEs may tend to subcontract a greater or lower proportion of their requirements of intermediates. Among the empirical studies, Cohen (1975) in the case of export-oriented firms in Taiwan, South Korea and Singapore found that local firms had a greater degree of vertical integration. Newfarmer and Marsh (1981), and Willmore (1986), found a reverse pattern in the case of Brazil. UNCTC (1981) could not find any significant difference between the extent of subcontracting of a foreign subsidiary and a local company in India both producing trucks. Therefore, no definite pattern emerges from the existing work.

We shall compare the degree of vertical integration (VAS_i) of foreign and local firms in our sample of Indian manufacturing without making a prediction.

VAS_i Value added as a proportion of total net sales of ith group of firms in 1980–81.

Export Performance

Being a part of multinational enterprises, FCEs enjoy several advantages over their local counterparts in export markets. These include a captive access to market information networks, marketing outlets, brand loyalty, etc. Hence, other things being the same, FCEs are better equipped to tap export markets than their local counterparts (de la Torre, Jr. 1974; Helleiner 1976). MNEs have evidently played an important role in the rapid expansion of manufactured exports of some Southeast Asian countries during the 1970s (Nayyar 1978; Lall 1980b). The decision to export from the host country, however, is an important aspect of the global strategy of the enterprise. Hence, the relative export performance of FCEs may be determined more by their global corporate strategy than by export advantages.

In India's case there have been additional reasons for expecting a better export performance by FCEs than their local counterparts. In addition to general export incentives, FCEs have been encouraged by the government to export through both direct and indirect means. Under the provisions of FERA (1973) foreign firms were permitted to retain a higher level (51 or 74 per cent) of foreign equity than the general ceiling of 40 per cent if they manufactured predominantly for the export market. Expansion into industrial activities, otherwise not open to FCEs with over 40 per cent foreign equity (such as non-core sectors or those reserved for the small-scale sector), was permitted in cases of production for export. Further, the government sometimes imposed export obligations on foreign collaboration approvals or on industrial licences to foreign controlled firms for expansion/diversification. It is evident that roughly 20 per cent of foreign collaborations approved between 1974 and 1978 had certain export obligations (Gulati and Bansal 1980).

The findings of empirical studies comparing export performance of FCEs and local firms in different countries have been mixed. Based on a study of export-oriented firms in South Korea, Taiwan, and Singapore, Cohen (1975) concluded that local firms were more likely to export than foreign firms, while Reidel (1975) found no significant difference in export performance of the two groups of firms in Taiwan (except in the case of electronics). Some studies compared the proportion of exports in sales of firms predominantly producing for domestic markets, and found that foreign controlled firms performed relatively poorly. The examples include, Lall and Streeten (1977), and Subrahmanian and Pillai (1979), for India; Jenkins (1979) for Mexico; Kirim (1986) for the Turkish pharmaceutical industry; and Solomon and Ingham (1977) for the British mechanical industry. Studies by Morgenstern and Muller (1976) for 10 Latin American countries; Newfarmer and Marsh (1981) for the Brazilian electric equipment industry; and Fairchild and Sosin (1986) also for Latin American countries, could not find any significant difference. Lall and Mohammad (1983b) found a positive, though weak, influence of degree of foreign ownership on industry's export performance in India. But that does not necessarily imply a superior export performance of FCEs compared to their local counterparts. Furthermore, in their study the influence of foreign ownership appeared to be significant only in the absence of another independent variable with which it was collinear.

We shall examine whether FCEs export a significantly higher proportion of their turnover (EXP_i) than their local counterparts in Indian manufacturing industries.

EXP_i Exports as a proportion of net sales of ith group of firms in 1980–81.

Financial Policy and Tax Planning

The proportion of retained earnings in disposable profits (retention ratio), and the ratio of borrowings to shareholders' funds (leverage ratio), are considered the two central financial policy decisions of firms (Hay and Morris 1979, ch. 10). These two together determine the valuation ratio and cost of obtaining funds for the firm. Tax planning (of corporate income) is also an important aspect of financial strategy because it influences the volume of cash flow and the effective cost of investments. The behaviour of FCEs and LCEs will be compared in terms of these three components of financial strategy.

Retention Behaviour

Apart from influencing the market valuation of a firm's stock, the retention versus pay out behaviour of the corporate sector is an important parameter of the saving/investment situation in the country. Since the retention ratio determines the valuation of a firm's capital, it is subject to a stock market constraint (Marris 1964). A high retention ratio and consequently a low pay out ratio may lead to a decline in the market valuation of the firm. A very low stock price may not only affect the flow of external funds to it but may also activate bulls to mount a take over raid. FCEs may be less susceptible to this constraint as big chunks of share capital held by the foreign share holders are not traded locally. Given the stock market constraint, the retention versus pay out decision of FCEs may be influenced by, among other things, the relative attractiveness of investment in the host country, investment opportunities, proportion and pattern of distribution of local share holdings, and the parent's perception of the role of affiliates in its global strategy. These factors vary from firm to firm. No *a priori* reasoning for expecting a difference in the retention ratios of FCEs and local firms in any particular manner is possible. Jo (1980) found FCEs to retain a significantly lower proportion of profits than their local counterparts. In his exercise, however, the extraneous factors had not been controlled for. The retention behaviour (REP_i) of two groups of firms will be compared here without making any prediction.

REP_i Retained earnings of ith group of firms as a proportion of total profit after tax in the year 1980–81.

Financing Pattern

The proportion of borrowed funds in the financing of capital requirements determines the cost of funds for the firm. FCEs have an additional incentive to depend more on the locally raised loans because this reduces their exposure to exchange risk. Their better credit-worthiness and strong financial position ensure a flow of the desired volume of funds to them. On the other hand, higher cash flow on account of their hypothesized higher profitability may reduce their borrowing requirements. The findings of the empirical studies are mixed. Subrahmanian (1972) found FCEs to depend less on borrowed funds than their local counterparts in nine of the 12 pairs of firms studied in India. Lall (1976) in the case of India, and Gershenberg and Ryan (1978) in the case of Uganda, could not find any significant difference in the borrowing requirements of FCEs. Here again, the leverage ratio (LEV_i) of FCEs and their local counterparts will be compared without making any firm prediction.

LEV_i Total long-term borrowings of ith group of firms as a proportion of net worth in 1980–81.

Tax Planning

Rates of corporate income tax in India are generally high. However, to encourage investments a number of concessions are permitted, such as a tax holiday for new investment, accelerated depreciation, and allowances like investment allowance and weighted deductions. Therefore, the effective rate of tax applicable to a company becomes a function of tax planning which can even reduce the tax liability of an otherwise profitable company to an insignificant sum. Another factor which might influence the effective rates of tax is profitability. Though the prescribed rates of tax are flat (a slightly higher rate for closely-held companies and a lower rate for widely-held companies), an element of progression has been brought in by imposing a surtax for companies earning supernormal profits. One might expect that FCEs may be at a disadvantage compared to local firms in their ability to reduce tax liability, being as they are, alien to the land. Second, the supposedly high profitability of their operations might attract surtax. Both factors will lead the effective tax rate for FCEs to be higher. Therefore, the effective rate of tax (ERT_i) for FCEs can be expected to be higher than their local counterparts.

ERT_i Provision for tax made by ith group of companies as a proportion of profit before tax, in 1980–81.

Financial Management

Two aspects of financial management—inventory management and liquidity—are considered here for the purposes of comparison.

Inventory Management

A certain amount of inventory is necessary for running production processes in manufacturing activity. However, large accumulation of inventory adds to the cost of capital. Inventory management, therefore, is an important indicator of the efficiency of marketing and procurement networks. Since possession of efficient management and organizational skills is considered to be one of the intangible assets held by MNEs, one can expect FCEs to be able to manage with a smaller volume of inventory per unit of sales compared to their local counterparts. The performance of FCEs has not yet been compared with that of their local counterparts in terms of this aspect of managerial efficiency. In the absence of any empirical evidence we shall prefer to go by the expectation that FCEs' inventory requirements per unit of sales (INS_i) are lower.

INS_i Ratio of inventory to net sales of ith group of firms in the year 1980–81.

Liquidity

In addition to holding the necessary volume of inventory a

manufacturing firm needs liquidity to cover the lag between input procurement and recovery of sales proceeds. This requirement of liquid assets is referred to as working capital. Having a bearing on the total capital employed, and hence on cost, working capital management is an important aspect of financial management. Furthermore, a firm with a comfortable liquidity position may obtain a competitive advantage over its rivals by offering liberal suppliers' credits. Liquidity requirements of a firm may also depend upon the efficiency of the procurement and distribution channels. The reasons for differences between the liquidity positions of FCEs and local firms are not quite clear, nor are there any empirical studies on this aspect. Therefore, the relative liquidity position of FCEs and local firms will be compared without any *a priori* prediction. Liquidity is defined as the difference between current assets and current liabilities. Hence, it is measured by the current ratio (CUR_i)

CUR_i Ratio of current assets to current liabilities of ith group of firms in the year 1980–81.

Empirical Analysis

The empirical analysis includes comparisons of FCEs and LCEs in terms of the 15 parameters identified above. Table 4.1 summarizes the predictions formulated for each of the 15 parameters (indicated by a mark of interrogation (?) where no clear prediction is possible). Table 4.1 also presents means and standard deviations of the variables for FCEs and LCEs for 49 Indian manufacturing industries (43 industries in the case of FCEs as they had no representation in six of them). A look at the means reveals that for variables, Size, ADS, RDS, PCM, HIE, IMP, and ERT the mean differences are in accordance with the predictions. In the case of three variables, LKR, EXP, and INS, the differences are contrary to the expectations, in particular a higher LKR for FCEs. But the difference may not be statistically significant because the standard deviation of LKR is high for FCEs. On average, FCEs export a lower proportion of their sales and have a higher inventory per unit of sales, compared to local firms. Among the variables

Table 4.1
Parameters for Discriminating Foreign and Local Firms in Indian Manufacturing

Parameter	*Prediction*	*Mean (S.D.)*	
		FCEs	*LCEs*
Market structure, behaviour and performance			
1. Scale of operations	$SIZE_F > SIZE_L$	2887.19	1460.05
		(2985.5)	(1832.24)
2. Advertising intensity	$ADS_F > ADS_L$	.46	.33
		(.55)	(.45)
3. R&D intensity	$RDS_F < RDS_L$	.07	.106
		(.19)	(.15)
4. Profit margins	$PCM_F > PCM_L$	.096	.050
		(.053)	(.045)
5. Growth rate ($GROW_i$)	?	1.837	1.929
		(0.428)	(0.415)
Choice of technique			
6. Wages: capital ratio	$LKR_F < LKR_L$	0.399	0.299
		(0.499)	(0.204)
Employee compensation/ qualitative differences in employee skills			
7. Proportion of high-income employees in total wage bill	$HIE_F > HIE_L$	0.112	0.067
		(0.064)	(0.023)
Vertical inter-firm linkage generation			
8. Degree of import dependence	$IMP_F > IMP_L$	0.135	0.101
		(0.155)	(0.085)
9. Degree of vertical integration (VAS_i)	?	0.382	0.319
		(0.091)	(0.104)
Export performance			
10. Proportion of exports in sales	$EXP_F > EXP_L$	0.042	0.052
		(0.042)	(0.062)
Financial policy and tax planning			
11. Retention ratio (REP_i)	?	0.515	0.941
		(0.619)	(1.094)
12. Leverage ratio (LEV_i)	?	0.955	2.561
		(1.027)	(7.46)
13. Effective tax rate	$ERT_F > ERT_L$	0.537	0.266
		(0.356)	(0.805)
Financial management			
14. Inventory management	$INS_F < INS_L$	0.308	0.289
		(0.121)	(0.099)
15. Liquidity (CUR_i)	?	2.365	2.142
		(0.663)	(0.636)

Note: The means and standard deviations are based on 43 observations in the case of FCEs and 49 observations in the case of LCEs.

for which we do not have a definite prediction, the mean for FCEs is higher in the case of VAS and CUR indicating their greater degree of vertical integration and richer liquidity position on average. FCEs have a lower mean in the case of GROW, LEV, and REP.

Examination of the statistical significance of these mean differences is conducted in two stages. In the first stage the univariate tests of significance of the differences are performed. The findings of the univariate tests may sometimes be misleading because they do not take into account the interaction among the discriminating variables. In the second stage, therefore, the variables found to be important discriminators in the univariate test are considered simultaneously in a multivariate framework.

Stage I: Univariate Analysis

The univariate test applied here is non-parametric. Non-parametric tests have the advantage of not assuming any specific distribution of the population under analysis. Hence they are uniquely suited to behavioural sciences data. Among the various non-parametric tests, the Wilcoxon Matched-Pairs Signed-Rank Test is one of the more powerful ones, as it utilizes information on both the direction and the magnitude of the differences within pairs. It gives more weight to a pair that shows a large difference than to a pair that shows a smaller difference. It has been used for similar purposes by Mason (1973), Willmore (1976), Agarwal (1979), and Chung and Lee (1980). For more than 25 observations, T (the test statistics) is normally distributed with

$$\text{mean} = \frac{n'(n'+1)}{4}\ ; \ \text{variance} = \frac{n'(n'+1)(2n'+1)}{24}$$

where n is the number of non-zero differences (see Siegel 1956, for more details). Hence standard normal variate Z can be calculated by dividing the difference between T and its mean by its standard deviation.

Since six of the 49 industries in our data base have no representation of FCEs, we shall confine our analysis to the

43 matched pairs of industries. The test can be, as usual, either one- or two-tailed. Since in a few cases we have no definite prediction about the sign of T, we shall use the latter. The findings of the Wilcoxon's test are presented in Table 4.2. It is apparent that of the 15 variables employed, differences between FCEs and LCEs are statistically significant only in the case of 10 variables at the 5 per cent or higher level (two-tailed).

Table 4.2
Analysis of Discriminating Characteristics: Findings of Wilcoxon's Signed-Rank Test

Parameter	*Z Statistics*	*Level of statistical significance (two-tailed test)*	*Inference*
1. SIZE	3.223	1%	$SIZE_F > SIZE_L$
2. ADS	0.78 1.37*	—	
3. RDS	2.35	5%	$RDS_F < RDS_L$
4. PCM	4.334	1%	$PCM_F > PCM_L$
5. GROW	2.34	5%	$GROW_F < GROW_L$
6. LKR	1.468	—	
7. HIE	4.429	1%	$HIE_F > HIE_L$
8. IMP	0.58 0.343*	—	
9. VAS	4.13	1%	$VAS_F > VAS_L$
10. EXP	0.78 0.587*	—	
11. REP	4.167	1%	$REP_F < REP_L$
12. LEV	3.128	1%	$LEV_F < LEV_L$
13. ERT	2.196	5%	$ERT_F > ERT_L$
14. INS	0.657	—	
15. CUR	2.149	5%	$CUR_F > CUR_L$

Notes: (*a*) Number of observations are 43 matched pairs of industries in all the cases; (*b*) an asterisk indicates results obtained for weighted averages of the respective variable; (*c*) inferences are subject to verification in the multivariate tests.

Of the five variables representing different aspects of market structure and performance, four (SIZE, RDS, PCM, and GROW) were significant. The direction of differences suggests that FCEs have significantly larger scales of operation and enjoy higher profit margins than their local counterparts. This result is in line with the general impression and the hypotheses formulated above. These findings also indicate that FCEs spend a relatively smaller proportion of their income on R&D and seem to be growing at a slower rate than their local counterparts. However, one needs to control for the possible interaction among variables before reaching a final conclusion.

The analysis fails to bring out any significant differences in the intensity of advertisement expenditures of FCEs and LCEs. It is possible that FCEs spend significantly more on advertising in advertising intensive industries. Thus, giving equal weight to all industries may not be appropriate. To correct for this the advertising intensity of FCEs and LCEs is weighted for the industry's share in total advertising expenditure by the sample firms. Though weighting improves the Z statistics from 0.84 to 1.37, it continues to remain insignificant. In view of the MNE's predisposition towards product differentiation, advertising intensity of FCEs was expected to be more than that of LCEs. This result, however, does not rule out any impact of FCEs on this aspect of market structure. As indicated earlier, it is possible that penetration of MNEs in an industry induces the firms to adopt a non-price mode of rivalry, which increases the general level of advertising activity in the industry. The only way of checking this is to examine the dynamic pattern of advertising behaviour of industry firms *vis-à-vis* the entry of FCEs. Moreover, FCEs enjoy access to intangible assets and hence, are able to internalize the benefits of a part of the advertising done by their parent and associate firms in the rest of the world (Connor and Mueller 1982). Hence, the current advertising expenditure of FCEs may yield proportionately higher returns than that of LCEs. Another reason why FCEs may be getting more mileage out of the same proportion of income spent on advertising could be due to economies of scale. FCEs have been found to have significantly larger scales of operation. Hence, the scale of their advertising is larger than that of LCEs.

The factor proportions of FCEs are also not significantly different from those of LCEs. However, caution needs to be used in interpreting results pertaining to this variable because of the limitations of measurement. The difference in terms of the proportion of high income employees (HIE) is significant at the one per cent level. This finding, however, is subject to confirmation in multivariate tests.

Of the two sources of vertical local inter-firm linkages compared, FCEs' behaviour is not significantly different in terms of import dependence. The difference continues to remain insignificant even if the import dependence of FCEs and LCEs is weighted for the industry's share in total imports by the sample firms. Most of the studies done for other countries found FCEs to have a tendency to import a higher proportion of raw materials and intermediate goods than local firms. In India's case this result may be an outcome of strict exchange and import regulations, and the high priority attached to import substitution. In addition to quantitative restrictions on imports and high tariffs, the government's tendency to canalize most of the bulk imports may have contributed to this result. The behaviour of FCEs regarding the 'make or buy' decision is significantly different, as revealed by the higher degree of vertical integration (VAS).

The export orientation of FCEs does not seem to be significantly different from their local counterparts. Again, weighting of export performance by industry's share in total exports of the sample firms makes no difference to the result. It indicates that FCEs in India are largely local market oriented. In view of its importance, the relative export behaviour of FCEs in Indian manufacturing will be analysed at a greater length in chapter 6.

The aspects of an enterprise's financial policy considered here, namely, retention and leverage ratios, are significant in discriminating between FCEs and LCEs. This suggests a lower propensity on the part of FCEs to retain profits and to depend on external sources of financing. The tax-planning variable is also significant and has the hypothesized sign.

Of the two aspects of financial management, liquidity and inventory management, only the former is significant in differentiating the two groups of firms. FCEs appear to have greater liquidity than their local counterparts but do not reveal significantly different inventory behaviour compared to them. Inventory requirements are also dependent upon the degree of vertical integration (Hay and Morris 1979, ch. 15). The fact that FCEs do not require a significantly larger volume of inventory than the LCEs, in spite of the greater degree of vertical integration of their operations, might indicate the efficiency of their inventory management.

Stage II: Multivariate Analysis

The univariate analysis of statistical significance of differences has identified 10 of the 15 variables used as possible discriminants. These are: SIZE, PCM, RDS, GROW, HIE, VAS, REP, LEV, ERT, and CUR. In order to take into account the possible interaction among them the significance of mean differences will now be examined in the multivariate framework with the help of step-wise discriminant analysis. Discriminant analysis involves the fitting of linear discriminant score functions on the basis of observed data on a number of discriminating variables of individuals whose group membership is known. These functions (sometimes known as classification functions) can classify further cases into groups on the basis of values of discriminating variables (see Tatsuoka 1971; Klecka 1980; and Jackson 1983). In our case discriminant analysis can be used to examine whether FCEs differ from their local counterparts, and if so, in terms of which characteristics. Riedel (1975), Solomon and Forsyth (1977), and Solomon and Ingham (1977), have made use of discriminant analysis for similar purposes.

The discriminant score functions estimated are of the form:

$$Y_i = \beta_{io} + \beta_{i1} X_{i1} + \ldots + \beta_{in} X_{in} \qquad (4.1)$$

where Y_i is the discriminant score for i=FCEs, LCEs; X_{ij} is the jth discriminating variable (for j=1 to n); and β_{ij} is a coefficient.

An individual observation is classified into the group for which the discriminant score on the basis of its observed values is higher. The goodness of fit is judged in terms of the significance of the mean difference between groups which can be expressed as a F-ratio, and the ability of the fitted discriminant functions in correctly classifying the individual cases.

The discriminant analysis has three assumptions. First, no variable may be a linear combination of other discriminating

Table 4.3

Within Groups Correlation Matrix

	SIZE	PCM	ERT	REP	LEV	CUR	VAS	RDS	HIE	GROW
SIZE	1.0000									
PCM	–.2412	1.0000								
ERT	0.1537	0.0937	1.0000							
REP	–.0343	–.0983	0.1313	1.0000						
LEV	–.0361	–.3743	0.0021	0.0109	1.0000					
CUR	–.2524	–.0153	0.0106	–.0416	–.0121	1.0000				
VAS	–.2478	0.3195	0.0886	0.0336	0.0203	–.1461	1.0000			
RDS	–.0428	0.0926	–.0619	0.2057	–.0227	–.1234	0.1512	1.0000		
HIE	0.0490	0.1928	–.0900	0.0509	–.1092	0.0012	–0.0243	0.0597	1.0000	
GROW	–.0716	0.2853	–.0404	–.0141	–.1975	–.1635	–.0649	.0560	–.0853	1.0000

variable. Second, the population co-variance matrices are similar for each group. Third, each group is drawn from a population which has a multivariate normal distribution. It has been shown, however, that discriminant analysis is a rather robust technique and can tolerate some deviation from these assumptions (Klecka 1980; Jackson 1983). In our case, since data is drawn from the same set of industries (43 for FCEs and 49 for LCEs) for both groups the covariance matrices are expected to be identical.

Since all the 10 variables may not prove to be good discriminators, a step wise procedure is used to select the significant ones. The procedure begins by selecting the individual variable which provides the greatest univariate discrimination (in terms of groups mean difference or partial F-ratio or F to enter). It then pairs the first variable with each of the remaining variables to locate the combination which produces the greatest discrimination. The variable which contributes to the best pair is selected. In the third step, the procedure goes on to combine the first two with each of the remaining variables to form triplets. The best triplet determines the third variable to be entered, and so on. The step-wise procedure produces an optimal—not necessarily the best—set of discriminating variables (Klecka 1980).[4]

Table 4.3 presents a 'within groups correlation matrix' on all the 10 potential discriminating variables included in our analysis. Each correlation coefficient in this matrix is an estimate of the degree of relationship between the corresponding pair of variables *within the groups*, usually different from the total correlation, which is influenced by the differences. No two variables are found to be highly correlated so as to violate the assumption of the analysis.

Table 4.4 provides a summary of the step-wise procedure and variables selected with their relative contribution to the discrimination in terms of their partial F-ratio (F to enter or remove), and total F-ratio. According to this procedure only five of the 10 variables are found to be significant (at 5 per cent or higher level in terms of partial F-ratio) discriminants, namely SIZE, PCM, HIE, VAS, and CUR. The other five RDS, GROW, LEV, REP, and ERT, are not significant in the multivariate context. These variables might be good discriminators on their own, but they do not add to the discriminating information contributed by the significant variables. Hence their unique contributions to the analysis are inadequate. They are, therefore, excluded from the subsequent analysis. The total F-value at the fifth step indicates that the two groups indeed differ significantly (at the one per cent level). The estimated discriminant score functions with five selected discriminating variables are as follows:

For the FCEs,

$$Y_F = -26.4268 + .00165\ SIZE + 17.51979\ PCM + 8.42489\ CUR + 55.5710\ VAS + 46.8183\ HIE \quad (4.2)$$

and for the LCEs,

$$Y_L = -17.27061 + .00118\ SIZE + .73003\ PCM + 7.25883\ CUR + 47.57733\ VAS + 30.24234\ HIE. \quad (4.3)$$

Table 4.4
Summary of Step-wise Procedure of Discriminant Analysis

Step	*Discriminating variable entered*	*F to enter or remove (degree of freedom)*	*No. of variables included*	*Cumulative F-ratio (degrees of freedom)*
1.	HIE	21.3797* (1,90)	1	21.3796* (1,90)
2.	PCM	10.6548* (1,89)	2	17.1639* (2,89)
3.	SIZE	9.3042* (1,88)	3	15.6116* (3,88)
4.	VAS	4.8323* (1,87)	4	13.426* (4,87)
5.	CUR	6.8900* (1,86)	5	12.8466* (5,86)
6.	REP	1.8914 (1,85)	6	11.1319* (6,85)
7.	ERT	0.7149 (1,84)	7	9.6115* (7,84)
8.	RDS	0.4763 (1,83)	8	8.4172* (8,83)
9.	LEV	0.1493 (1,82)	9	7.4219* (9,82)
10.	GROW	0.1143 (1,81)	10	6.6189* (10,81)

* indicates significant at 5 per cent or above level.

It can be seen from Table 4.5 that the discriminant functions are able to classify nearly 85 per cent of observations correctly. Hence, they appear to be good fits.

Table 4.5
Classification Matrix

Actual group	*Classification*		*Total*	*Percentage of cases correctly classified*
	Foreign	*Local*		
Foreign	35	8	43	81.39
Local	6	43	49	87.75
Correctly classified	35	43	92	84.78

The findings of the discriminant analysis suggest that of the five parameters of market structure, conduct, and performance, only SIZE and PCM are able to distinguish FCEs and LCEs significantly. Both these findings are in tune with our hypotheses and corroborate the findings of a number of previous empirical studies. FCEs enjoy higher profit margins independent of their larger scales of operation (SIZE). The theoretical and empirical explanation of this difference in profitability performance needs to be examined in greater detail (see chapter 5).

The R&D intensity and growth rates which were found to be significantly different in the case of the univariate test are no longer able to distinguish the FCEs from their local counterparts in the multivariate case. The growth rates were perhaps influenced by scale of operation and not by foreign ownership. Therefore, when scale of operation was controlled for, the significance of growth rate variation vanished. R&D intensity's interaction is, however, not so clear.

The proportion of high income employees (HIE) continues to be a significant discriminant. In fact, this variable explains the maximum variation between the two groups. HIE could be higher in the case of FCEs due either to their tendency to employ more talented personnel or to their general tendency to pay their employees better. Which of the two tendencies is dominant, however, is not clear. For this purpose we analyse the inter-industry determinants of HIE as follows:

In the single equation framework,

$$HIE = \underset{(0.09)}{.0548} + \underset{(1.83)}{.049}\,FS + \underset{(1.35)}{.159}\,CR4 + \underset{(1.12)}{.095}\,PMS + \underset{(0.58)}{.015}\,ADS + \underset{(0.99)}{.021}\,RDS + \underset{(4.37)}{.718}\,SKIL_1 + \underset{(1.30)}{.033}\,PCM$$

$$R^2 = 0.59 \quad F = 8.60 \quad N = 49 \qquad (4.4)$$

In the simultaneous equation framework,

$$HIE = \underset{(.38)}{-.270} + \underset{(0.43)}{.019}\,FS^* + \underset{(1.45)}{.175}\,CR4 + \underset{(1.14)}{.098}\,PMS + \underset{(0.75)}{.021}\,ADS + \underset{(0.65)}{.014}\,RDS + \underset{(4.19)}{.798}\,SKIL_1 + \underset{(1.50)}{.041}\,PCM$$

$$R^2 = 0.57 \quad F = 7.91 \quad N = 49 \qquad (4.5)$$

where FS is the share of FCEs in industry sales; CR4 is the four-firm concentration ratio; PMS is the plant and machinery to sales ratio; ADS is the advertisement to sales ratio; RDS is the R&D to sales ratio; $SKIL_1$ is the proportion of overhead employees in total work force; and PCM is the price cost margin. Figures in parentheses are t-values. An asterisk indicates an endogenous variable.

Of the seven possible explanatory variables included in the equation (see Kumar 1986, for reasoning), only skill intensity and foreign share turn out to be significant determinants of HIE with positive signs in the single equation framework. But the relationship between HIE and FS is subject to a simultaneity bias as the former has been found to be a significant determinant of the latter ($SKIL_2$ in chapter 3). When the simultaneity of their relationship was sought to be controlled for (by integrating Equation 4.4 with equation (*i*) of Table 3.3) through two-stage least squares, the significance of FS vanished and only $SKIL_1$ remained a significant explanatory variable. The high proportion of high income employees in the case of FCEs, thus, appears to be on account of their tendency to employ qualitatively superior personnel than their local counterparts, as observed by Balasubramanyam (1984) in the case of Indonesia, and Willmore (1986) in Brazil. However, more detailed micro-level research is needed on this aspect before a definitive statement can be made. The FCE's tendency to employ qualitatively superior personnel may be an aspect of non-price rivalry and may lend them a formidable competitive advantage in skill intensive industries. It can also be a source of contrived entry barrier.

The degree of vertical integration (VAS) of FCEs is significantly greater than that of their local counterparts. This suggests that operations of FCEs generate fewer vertical inter-firm domestic linkages than do LCEs. The government policy of encouraging subcontracting to generate inter-firm linkages, therefore, seems to have found less favour with FCEs. The generation of linkages constitutes a boost to the development of the local industries. The performance of FCEs in this respect, therefore, appears to be inferior to that of LCEs.

The aspects of a firm's financial strategy, namely retention and leverage behaviour (REP and LEV), and the tax planning behaviour (ERT), are also not significant discriminators in the multivariate context. It appears that these variables are influenced more by the scale of operation and profit margin than by the nationality of ownership of the firm.

CUR is significant even in the multivariate context, which suggests that FCEs enjoy richer long-term sources of financing their current assets. The comfortable liquidity position which FCEs enjoy is independent of their larger scales of operations and their higher profit margins. They might be using their strong working capital position as a source of competitive advantage.

Industrial Variation in Group Characteristics

The above analysis suggests that, compared to local firms, FCEs in Indian manufacturing have significantly larger scales of operations, enjoy higher profit margins, are more vertically integrated and cash rich, and have better paid personnel. This, however, is a general picture. Some industry variation in the relative characteristics of foreign and local firms does exist as indicated by the misclassification of some cases by the discriminant functions. Table 4.5 indicates that 14 of the 92 observations were misclassified. FCEs in eight industries and LCEs in six industries do not wear the respective group's characteristics as specified by the discriminant functions on the basis of the whole sample. Table 4.6 lists names of the industries along with the foreign shares and the posterior probabilities of classification in particular groups where misclassifications have occurred. Five of the eight cases where FCEs have been misclassified are those where FCEs are of only marginal significance with their combined shares in industry sales under 10 per cent, namely, breweries and distilleries, steel forgings, foundries and engineering workshops, cement, and paper and board products. In these industries, a few FCEs that continue to exist are there for historical reasons. They seem to enjoy no competitive edge and hence, their characteristics do not reflect the distance that FCEs maintain from their local counterparts in other industries. In fact, market power in these sectors is in the hands of certain local companies affiliated to large local industrial conglomerates, such as United Breweries and Mohan Meakins in breweries and distilleries; Bihar Alloy Steel (Birla) in forgings; Mukand Iron, FACOR (Ferro Alloys Corporation), and Tata Yodogawa in foundries; ACC (Associated Cement Companies) in cement; and Central Pulp Mills in paper and board products. In the other three industries—metal products, paints and varnishes, and industrial and medical gases—although FCEs still enjoy substantial market shares their behaviour does not appear to be very different from that of their local counterparts.

All the six cases where LCEs have been misclassified, perhaps with the exception of industrial and medical gases, have one thing in common: LCEs in these industries are relatively large firms affiliated with large local industrial conglomerates and with technology imported under licensing. With the goodwill back- up of the parent (local) business house and technology from western MNEs they have almost matched the asset bundle of FCEs and hence, have a close resemblance to them in terms of the discriminating characteristics. For instances, Tata Engineering and Locomotive Company, Hindustan Motors, and Bajaj Auto in motor vehicles; Mysore Kirloskar in machine tools; J.K. Synthetics, Baroda Rayon, Indian Organic Chemicals, and Nirlon Synthetic Fibres in man-made fibres; Hyderabad Asbestos in asbestos and asbestos cement; and Modi Continental Tyres in automotive tyres and tubes.

Table 4.6
Misclassified Observations by the Discriminant Functions

Actual Group		*Industry*	*Posterior probability of misclassification*	*Share of FCEs in sales (FS)*
FCEs				
1.	370	Breweries and distilleries	.906	3.04
2.	454	Steel forgings	.511	5.05
3.	455	Foundries and engineering workshops	.505	7.54
4.	456–7	Metal products (n.e.s.)	.665	69.64
5.	467	Paints and varnishes	.629	52.13
6.	521	Cement	.967	5.24
7.	552	Products of paper and board	.840	6.76
8.	630	Industrial and medical gases	1.000	63.13
LCEs				
1.	441	Motor vehicles	.885	19.45
2.	449	Machine tools	.688	35.08
3.	463	Man-made fibres	.832	17.83
4.	522	Asbestos and A. cement	.545	43.78
5.	541	Auto tyres and tubes	.564	60.13
6.	630	Industrial and medical gases	.538	63.13

Note: n.e.s.=not elsewhere specified

Conclusions

This chapter has examined the firm characteristics that distinguish FCEs from their local counterparts. The analysis of discriminating characteristics is important for evaluating the indirect effects of the operations of FCEs (which may sometimes be considerable) in host developing countries. The current state of knowledge on this aspect was found to be deficient in many respects.

The distinguishing characteristics considered here included 15 diverse aspects of firms' conduct and performance. The statistical significance of the variables in actually discriminating the two groups of firms was examined for the sample of 49 three-digit Indian manufacturing industries in both univariate and multivariate frameworks. The findings of multivariate analysis indicate that a number of characteristics discriminate between FCEs and LCEs only on account of extraneous factors. Hence, the findings of studies made in a univariate context need a fresh look.

Among the different aspects of market structure, behaviour, and performance only larger scale of operations and higher profit margins (on sales) distinguished FCEs from their local counterparts. Their advertising intensity was not found to be significantly different from that of local firms. They might, however, still enjoy an edge over their counterparts in this respect, on account of internalization of a part of the goodwill generated by advertising done by their associate companies and due to economies of scale in advertising. R&D intensity and the growth rate of FCEs were both found to be lower only in the univariate test. The factor proportions also did not appear to be different.

A significantly higher proportion of employees of FCEs are in the high income category. This appears to be on account of the tendency of FCEs to employ qualitatively superior personnel than their local counterparts. This tendency could be an aspect of non-price rivalry, particularly in skill-intensive industries, and a source of contrived entry barrier.

Among the two sources of vertical local inter-firm linkages, FCEs' behaviour with regard to 'import or procure-locally' does not significantly differ from that of their local counterparts. This finding could be an outcome of the strict foreign trade and exchange regulations exercised by the government. In terms of the other important source of linkages, 'make or buy', however, FCEs differ significantly from their local counterparts. FCEs have a higher degree of vertical integration and hence, their operations generate fewer inter-firm linkages. Despite their advantages in export markets, and various fiscal incentives and government policy regulations to induce them to export, the proportion of their output that the FCEs export is not significantly different from that of their local counterparts. A more detailed analysis of their relative export behaviour is made in chapter 6.

The behaviour of FCEs in terms of the retention ratio, dependence on external funds (leverage), or tax planning appears to be different only on account of extraneous factors rather than because of foreign ownership. FCEs enjoy a more comfortable liquidity position due to their better long-term sources of funding working capital. This position can be used to secure a competitive advantage through their ability to extend liberal (supplier's) credits. In terms of inventory management, however, their performance was not very different from that of their local counterparts.

The above analysis, therefore, brings out five major differences between foreign and local enterprises: the scale of operation, the profit margins, the proportion of employees in high income categories, the degree of vertical integration, and liquidity ratio. In a few industries, however, local firms affiliated with large local conglomerates with technology obtained by licensing from abroad closely resembled their foreign counterparts in all the dimensions covered here.

Further, as this exercise was conducted in a comparative static framework it does not bring out the dynamic influences of the entry of FCEs into an industry on different aspects of the conduct of local firms. Since firms in an industry mutually interact, the behaviour of local firms could be altered, through competitive and demonstration effects, by the very presence of foreign rivals (Willmore, 1986). For instance, the presence of FCEs could have raised the general standards of advertising and other modes of non-price rivalry in an industry. This aspect of the effects of FCEs can be captured through dynamic analysis.

Notes

1. Here again we shall confine ourselves to 49 of the 54 manufacturing industries included in the database for the empirical exercise.
2. Lim (1976) found capital utilization of FCEs to be more intensive in Malaysia. The difference, however, vanished when other factors were controlled for.
3. A comparison in terms of crude the proxies, sales: capital employed ratio and sales: wages did not reveal any significant differences.
4. The actual computer program used was BMD07—Stepwise Discriminant Analysis—Revised Version, 24 July 1969, Health Sciences Computing Facility, University of California, Los Angeles.

5

Determinants of Profitability of Foreign and Local Enterprises in Indian Manufacturing

Introduction

The findings of chapter 4 suggest that FCEs enjoy higher profit margins compared to their local counterparts. The differences in their financial performance persist even after controlling for the influence of other factors, such as size. The conventional market structure-conduct-performance (SCP) paradigm (see Bain 1956) relates profitability to the degree of seller concentration and the height of entry barriers (Caves 1964; Scherer 1970). The entry barriers are industry specific and are expected to protect all firms in the industry in proportion to their sales. Therefore, the original SCP framework does not help in explaining systematic intra-industry differences in profitability except on the basis of size. An extension of the SCP paradigm takes note of variations in intra-industry structure (Caves and Porter 1977; Porter 1979). In this context, we analyse the determinants of profit margins of FCEs and local firms to seek explanations for their differential profit performance.

This chapter first formulates testable hypotheses by examining the relevance of different theoretical paradigms for explaining intra-industry profitability differences in the present context. The empirical results are then presented and the findings summarized.

Intra-Industry Profitability Differences: Hypotheses

The Theory

The original SCP paradigm provides no explanation of intra-industry profitability differences except on the basis of firm size. Subsequent empirical studies also attempted to explain inter-firm differences in profitability in terms of their market share and/or size (Shepherd 1972; Gale 1972). Mancke (1974) questioned the convention of drawing inferences from possible correlations between profitability, market share, firm size, and growth because all these parameters are influenced by the magnitude of success of past investments. Mancke's stochastic model of inter-firm profitability differences, however, does not appear to be relevant in explaining systematic differences in profitability observed here in terms of nationality of ownership. Demsetz (1973), among others, attributes the inter-firm differences in profitability to possible inter-firm ability differences which may be due to the firms' possession of rent-yielding intangible assets. This explanation may fit in the present context as ownership of intangible assets is indeed a characteristic that explains the very existence of FCEs. Hence, it may be worth examining whether there are significant inter-group efficiency differences leading to superior profitability of FCEs.

A recent extension of the SCP paradigm provides an explanation for sustained inter-group differences in profitability in terms of the heterogeneity of firms in different groups (Caves and Porter 1977; Newman 1978; Porter 1979). According to this hypothesis an industry may be composed of one or more strategic groups of firms. The firms in a given strategic group recognize the mutual interdependence more closely than all the other firms in the industry. The entry barriers do not protect all firms equally. Sustained differences in profitability, therefore, are possible if one group of firms consistently enjoys greater protection from certain entry barriers than the others.

It is possible that FCEs and LCEs in Indian industries constitute different strategic groups. In what follows we briefly discuss the concept of strategic groups.

FCEs and LCEs as Two Strategic Groups

The concept of strategic groups is based on the commonplace observation that there are alternative ways of doing business in an industry and that the strategy of firms in any particular industry differs with respect to variables—besides scale of operation—such as mode of competitive rivalry, degree of vertical integration, geographical extent of markets served, nature of distribution channels employed, and breadth of product line (Porter 1979; Oster 1982). An industry, therefore, is composed of groups of firms, and firms in a group are similar to each other in terms of competitive strategy. Hence, they recognize mutual dependence more closely. One implication of the segmentation of industry into strategic groups is that entry barriers are partly specific to the strategic groups and partly to the industry (Porter 1979). The entry barriers not only impede fresh entry to the industry, but also restrict inter-strategic group mobility of existing firms and hence, are generally referred to as 'mobility barriers'. Thus, firms in a particular strategic group may not only enjoy protection from new entrants to the industry but also from existing firms belonging to other strategic groups in the same industry. The mobility barriers could be the source of persistent advantage and hence, might explain the higher profit margins enjoyed by some firms in an industry.

We shall now examine how far FCEs and local firms in Indian industries can be considered to belong to different strategic groups. The strategic differences between firms are, among other factors, reflections of their tangible and intangible assets (Porter 1979). In these respects, FCEs clearly stand out from their local rivals. As observed earlier, FCEs enjoy an access to intangible assets which lend them special advantages over purely national firms, such as brand goodwill, proprietary technology, captive access to the parent's research laboratories, reservoirs of organizational and managerial skills, and information networks. In addition, their affiliation with international chains of firms with centralized decision-making aiming at global optimization of resources/opportunities may also lead to strategic differences. These differences are reflected in terms of their significantly larger scales of operation, tendency to employ qualitatively superior manpower, higher degree of vertical integration, and high level of liquidity compared to their local counterparts (see chapter 4). Thus, there appears to be a reasonable case for treating FCEs as belonging to a strategic group different from that of their local counterparts in respective industries.

Hypotheses

The proposition that differential protection enjoyed from entry or mobility barriers is the source of higher profitability of FCEs can be verified by analysing the determinants of profitability of two groups of firms. If entry barriers protect FCEs and local firms differently, the relationships between profitability and market structural variables will be different for the two groups. We will specify the profit functions of FCEs and LCEs, which will then be estimated. In addition to differential protection from entry barriers, a part of the higher profit margins of FCEs may be due to their superior operational ability (Demsetz 1973). The inter-group ability differences, if any, should be reflected in different intercept terms of the profit functions. Hence, they can be detected by examining the intercept terms of the respective profit functions.

Empirical analyses of industry profitability in the SCP framework have estimated functional relationships between industry profitability and elements of market structure: the degree of seller concentration, height of entry barriers, and growth of industry demand. Typical relationships estimated in these studies are of the form:

$$PCM_T = f(\underset{+}{BARR}, \underset{+}{CR}, \underset{+}{GR}) \qquad (5.1)$$

where PCM_T is the industry price cost margin, BARR is a vector of different entry barriers, CR is the degree of seller concentration, and GR is the growth rate of industry demand. Signs indicate the nature of the relationships.

If PCM_F and PCM_L represent average profit margins for

FCEs and LCEs respectively, we could write their profit functions as:

$$PCM_F = f_1\,(BARR, \; CR, \; GR) \qquad (5.2)$$
$$PCM_L = f_2\,(BARR, CR, GR) \qquad (5.3)$$

The central prediction of the strategic group paradigm is that these functions will be different with respect to elements of BARR. The nature of the difference will be determined by the competitive strategies followed by the two groups of firms. We will now evaluate the possible nature of relationships between profit margins of the two groups of firms and the explanatory variables.

Entry or Mobility Barriers

Product Differentiation and Goodwill

In view of their possession of intangible assets, such as brand names enjoying consumer loyalty, FCEs can be expected to pursue competitive strategies based on non-price competition through product differentiation. A new entrant or even an existing local firm will need to undertake substantial advertising to match the brand goodwill enjoyed by FCEs cultivated through past and current advertising campaigns by them and their associates in India and elsewhere. FCEs, therefore, are expected to enjoy protection from a product differentiation entry barrier. Hence, a positive and significant relationship between PCM_F and ADS (advertising intensity) is predicted. The relationship between PCM_L and ADS, however, is not so clear. This is because among local firms there may be firms, particularly those affiliated to large industrial houses, also pursuing strategies dominated by product differentiation, while there may be others that concentrate on price-competition. The product differentiation mobility barrier may create an umbrella for local firms, and may also push up their profits to some extent (Porter 1979). The net effect of ADS on PCM_L may, therefore, depend upon inter-strategic group structure and on the viability of non-advertising intensive strategies (Caves and Pugel 1980). Hence, no precise prediction regarding the relationship between advertising intensity and PCM_L can be made. But the level of its significance should be lower than that in the case of PCM_F. The product differentiation entry barrier is captured through the advertising intensity (ADS) of industry.

ADS Advertising expenditure as a proportion of sales, averaged over three years: 1978–79 to 1980–81

Product differentiation through advertising is effective mainly in the case of consumer goods industries. Our sample of industries comprises both consumer as well as non-consumer goods industries. This heterogeneity needs to be controlled for. Following the common practice (Caves *et al.* 1980) we shall use a multiplicative slope dummy ADCON.

$$\text{ADCON} = \text{ADS} * \text{DCON}$$

where DCON is a consumer goods dummy, taking the value one for consumer goods industries and zero otherwise.

Knowledge Intensity

Two forms of knowledge intensity are considered here: the intensity of industry in technological (process or product technology) inputs, and in skills (organizational, managerial, and technical). The technology intensity barrier requires an entrant either to undertake R&D to generate technology, or to procure it from abroad. In view of the economies of scale in R&D activity and imperfections in the technology markets, technology intensity may become quite a formidable barrier. Intensity of the industry in managerial/technical skills, particularly in a developing economy like India with inelastic skill supplies, may again prove to be a strong barrier. Siddharthan and Dasgupta (1983) have noted its role in the Indian context. Bain (1956) covers these two sources of entry barriers under absolute cost advantage. These entry barriers could also be equally strong mobility barriers.

FCEs, because of their captive access to laboratories of the parent enterprise and to the reservoir of skills cultivated through their experience of operating similar plants in several countries, may enjoy better protection from both technology and skill entry barriers. Local firms with no such captive sources will either have to set up in-house R&D facilities to provide technological inputs or depend continuously on foreign sources. Otherwise even existing local firms run the risk of facing technological obsolescence. Similarly, in skill-intensive industries, local firms must be prepared to pay high salaries to attract and retain specialized personnel. Therefore, a positive and significant relationship between PCM_F and technology and skill intensities is predicted. Such a relationship is doubtful in the case of PCM_L.

In measuring the technology intensity (TECH) of an industry it is proposed to take into account both local and imported technology inputs.

TECH In-house R&D expenditure and remittances on account of royalty and technical fees as a proportion of net sales, averaged over three years: 1978–79 to 1980–81.

Skill intensity will be proxied through two alternative variables, namely, $SKIL_1$ and $SKIL_2$, (see chapter 3).

$SKIL_1$ Non-production workers as a proportion of the total work force in 1978–79.

$SKIL_2$ Earnings of high salaried employees (those receiving Rs 3,000 per month or more) as a proportion of the total wages and salaries bill, averaged over three years: 1978–79 to 1980–81.

Absolute Capital Requirements

High initial capital requirements for setting up an economic-size plant has been a standard barrier to new entry (Bain 1956). Its role as a mobility barrier, however, is not clear. Nevertheless, it will be interesting to examine how this entry barrier affects PCM_F and PCM_L. In the absence of information on economic size of plants in different industries, we shall use average capital requirements (per firm) as a proxy for absolute capital requirements(AKR).

AKR Total capital employed per firm, averaged over three years: 1978–79 to 1980–81.

Length of the Production Process or the Degree of Vertical Integration

The length of the production process or the degree of vertical integration necessary for running a business in an industry is an aspect which gives absolute cost advantage to existing firms. There are no reasons to expect that the vertical integration entry barrier would affect FCEs and LCEs differently. It may, in fact, be an industry specific entry barrier protecting both groups of firms. Hence, a positive relationship is predicted between the degree of vertical integration, and both PCM_F and PCM_L. The degree of vertical integration is proxied by VAS.

VAS Value added as a proportion of net sales, 1980–81.

Seller Concentration

High seller concentration makes collusion among the leading firms more effective (Strickland and Weiss 1976). From the evidence of their significantly larger size found in chapter 4, FCEs appear to be leading firms in their respective branches of industry. In such cases PCM_F may be positively related to the degree of seller concentration. The relationship between seller concentration and PCM_L is, however, ambiguous.

The degree of seller concentration is conventionally proxied through a four-firm concentration ratio (CR4). However, limitations of this measurement (as also of its alternative, the Herfindahl index) have been pointed out in the literature, for example, Phillips (1976). In view of the lack of a superior alternative and given the database, we shall use CR4.

CR4 Share of top four firms in net industry (sample) sales, averaged over three years: 1978–79 to 1980–81.

Growth of Demand

The rate of growth of industry demand has been posited to influence profit margins of industry firms favourably. The rate of growth is an industry specific factor; it does not discriminate between FCEs and LCEs. Hence, a positive influence is predicted on both PCM_F and PCM_L. Here again measurement of demand growth rate poses a problem. In the absence of a ready-made indicator, most studies have used the growth rate of industry output (GROW) as a proxy for industry demand. Though GROW has obvious limitations in representing the rate of growth of demand (Phillips 1976), in the absence of any better index we shall use it.

GROW Proportionate change in net industry sales over three years: 1978–79 to 1980–81.

Firm Size

Intra-industry differences in profitability can emerge due to differences in firm size. In order to control for the possible effect of differential firm size, the average firm size of FCEs and LCEs ($SIZE_i$) will be included in their respective profit functions. The firm size and profitability relationship is determined by two counteracting influences. Large firms may be able to reap economies of scale in production, advertising, marketing, and R&D. On the other hand, too large an organization may also suffer from diseconomies of scale and X-inefficiency. The relationship between PCM and firm size will depend upon the net outcome of these two influences.

$SIZE_i$ Average net sales per firm in group i in 1980–81; (i=FCE, LCE).

Capital Intensity

Since our dependent variable is the price cost margin and not the rate of return, the industry's capital intensity needs to be controlled for as per the standard practice. The capital intensity will be proxied through COR.

COR Total capital employed to net sales ratio, averaged over three years: 1978–79 to 1980–81.

International Trade

Several studies have treated international trade as an aspect of market structure and have included the extent of import competition and export-orientation while explaining variation in profitability. For example, Esposito and Esposito (1971); Khalilzadeh-Shirazi (1974); Pagoulatos and Sorensen (1976); Caves *et al.* (1980); Pugel (1980); and Melo and Urata (1986). In India's case, where exports constitute only a marginal fraction of the sample firm's output and import competition is restricted by tariffs and quota restrictions, it may not be of much consequence for profitability. Nevertheless, Katrak (1980), and Siddharthan and Dasgupta (1983), have considered it. The protection enjoyed by local industry from import competition may have a positive effect on PCM. On the other hand, the lack of competition may be associated with operational inefficiency, nullifying the favourable impact on profits. Nevertheless, effective rates of protection (ERP) would be employed to examine the influence of protection on PCM following Hitris (1978) and Katrak (1980).

ERP Effective rates protection as estimated by the NCAER, 1979–80.

The hypotheses formulated above can be summed up as follows:

$$PCM_F = f_1\ (\underset{+}{ADS},\ \underset{+}{ADCON},\ \underset{+}{TECH},\ \underset{+}{SKIL_1},\ \underset{+}{SKIL_2},\ \underset{+}{AKR},\ \underset{+}{VAS},\ \underset{+}{CR4},\ \underset{?}{SIZE_F},\ \underset{+}{GROW},\ \underset{+}{COR},\ \underset{+}{ERP}) \qquad (5.4)$$

$$PCM_L = f_2\ (\underset{*}{ADS},\ \underset{*}{ADCON},\ \underset{*}{TECH},\ \underset{*}{SKIL_1},\ \underset{*}{SKIL_2},\ \underset{+}{AKR},\ \underset{+}{VAS},\ \underset{*}{CR4},\ \underset{?}{SIZE_L},\ \underset{+}{GROW},\ \underset{+}{COR},\ \underset{+}{ERP}) \qquad (5.5)$$

The signs below each variable indicate the predicted sign of the coefficient. When the *a priori* reasoning is not clear about the relationship it has been indicated by (?). An asterisk below a variable in the PCM_L equation indicates that its sign/level of statistical significance is predicted to be different from that obtained from the corresponding variable in the PCM_F equation.

Following Collins and Preston (1970), and Khalilzadeh Shirazi (1974), PCM is defined as follows:

PCM_i Profit before tax of ith group of firms as a proportion of their net worth in 1980–81.

Empirical Analysis

To verify the hypotheses formulated above, Equations 5.4 and 5.5 were fitted for a sample of 43 Indian manufacturing industries. The regressions were fitted in the original form as well as on the logarithmic transformation of data. For reasons of 'goodness of fit' only those results pertaining to the logarithmic transformation are presented.[1]

Some indication of the differential effects of entry barriers on profitability of FCEs and LCEs is provided by the correlation matrix presented in Table 5.1. The correlation between PCM_F and PCM_L, though significant (r=0.405), is not very high. The correlations of ADS, ADCON, TECH, $SKIL_1$, $SKIL_2$ are quite significant with PCM_F, but are rather poor with PCM_L. Other variables, too, have different correlations with PCM_F and PCM_L.

The estimated regression equations explaining industry variation in PCM_F and PCM_L are presented in Table 5.2. Since variables CR4, GROW, COR, and ERP were never significant, they were excluded from the equations presented. The unimportance of CR4 and GROW may be because of the problems of measurement discussed earlier. They were also insignificant in a number of previous studies, such as Comanor and Wilson (1974), Esposito and Esposito (1971), Khalilzadeh-Shirazi (1974), and Siddharthan and Dasgupta (1983). Another explanation for the insignificance of CR4 and ERP could be that the positive effect which these variables might be having on profits is cancelled by the operational inefficiency resulting from the lack of competition. These two variables were significant, with a positive sign, in Katrak's (1980) study of Indian manufacturing. But his exercise related to the early 1960s and did not specify other elements of market structure, such as entry barriers.

An examination of the residuals revealed three 'outliers' for local firms and one for FCEs. Exclusion of these three outlying observations improved the goodness of fit of PCM_L equation as indicated by equation (3a) in Table 5.2. Exclusion of one outlier, however, made no improvement to the PCM_F equation.

Table 5.1
Correlation Matrix

(Log x Log)

	PCM_F	PCM_L	ADS	ADCON	TECH	$SKIL_1$	$SKIL_2$	AKR	VAS	COR	GROW	$SIZE_F$	$SIZE_L$	ERP	CR_4
PCM_F	1.00														
PCM_L	.405	1.00													
ADS	-.001	-.093	1.00												
ADCON	.513	.286	-.042	1.00											
TECH	.530	.211	-.128	.38	1.00										
$SKIL_1$	.391	.210	.016	.558	.558	1.00									
$SKIL_2$	.470	.047	.033	.52	.386	.665	1.00								
AKR	.006	.125	-.372	.163	.169	.190	.322	1.00							
VAS	.293	.162	.139	.204	.001	-.106	-.109	-.261	1.00						
COR	.326	.095	-.514	.15	.28	.031	.196	.300	.233	1.00					
GROW	.153	.067	-.089	.28	.25	.181	-.021	-.233	-.09	-.07	1.00				
$SIZE_F$	-.315	-.068	-.133	-.119	-.107	.173	.279	.711	-.318	-.183	-.271	1.00			
$SIZE_L$	.180	.415	-.258	.114	.319	.194	.152	.756	-.377	.158	-.019	.372	1.00		
ERP	-.135	-.236	.381	-.156	-.256	-.170	-.037	.051	.115	-.204	-.152	.201	-.073	1.00	
CR_4	.025	-.137	-.097	.29	-.291	.013	.037	.155	-.009	.062	-.193	-.005	-.016	.144	1.00
	PCM_F	PCM_L	ADS	ADCON	TECH	$SKIL_1$	$SKIL_2$	AKR	VAS	COR	GROW	$SIZE_F$	$SIZE_L$	ERP	CR_4

Table 5.2
Regression Equations Explaining Profit Margins of FCEs and LCEs

Independent variables	*Dependent variable*				
	PCM_F		PCM_L		
	1	*2*	*3*	*3a*	*4*
1. ADS	.0016	.015	–.189	–.169	–.181
	(.041)	(.376)	(.882)	(.797)	(.875)
2. ADCON	.070	.139	1.467	1.865	1.250
	(.307)	(.545)	(1.226)	(1.579)	(1.004)
3. TECH	.030^{c}	.038^{b}	–.070	–.108	–.062
	(1.967)	(2.432)	(.790)	(1.160)	(.750)
4. $SKIL_1$		.577^{c}			1.092
		(1.879)			(.719)
5. $SKIL_2$	.648^{a}		.574	.052	
	(2.933)		(.464)	(.040)	
6. AKR	.146	.170	–1.848^{a}	–1.959^{a}	–1.734^{a}
	(1.228)	(1.323)	(2.648)	(2.748)	(2.762)
7. VAS	.628^{c}	.623^{c}	4.587^{b}	5.344^{a}	4.648^{b}
	(1.962)	(1.806)	(2.413)	(2.812)	(2.497)
8. $SIZE_i$	–.268^{a}	–.234^{a}	2.945^{a}	3.728^{a}	2.838^{a}
	(2.672)	(2.202)	(4.284)	(4.845)	(4.428)
9. Intercept	2.680	1.812	–2.335	–4.907	–4.664
R^{-2}	.588	.534	.437	.506	.442
F	7.138^{a}	5.727^{a}	3.88^{a}	4.682^{a}	3.957^{a}
Sum of squared residuals	5.789	6.552	177.609	154.030	176.098
N	43	43	43	40	43

Note: Variables GROW, CR4, ERP and COR remained insignificant throughout, and hence, were dropped from equations reported here. Figures in parentheses are t-values. Superscripts indicate levels of significance as follows: (*a*) 1 per cent: (*b*) 5 per cent; and (*c*) 10 per cent (two-tailed test). While estimating equation 3a, three outliers were excluded from the sample.

The equations in Table 5.2 reveal important differences both in overall terms as well as concerning the performance of individual explanatory variables. At the overall level two important differences are noticed. First, while the seven variables included in these equations are able to explain nearly 60 per cent of variation in PCM_F, they explain only about 50 per cent of variation in PCM_L. The overall level of significance of the PCM_F equations in terms of F-tests is also higher than in the case of PCM_L. These differences imply that profit margins of local firms are much less determined by market structural factors than those of FCEs. Second, the intercept term, which is positive in PCM_F equations, has a negative sign in the case of PCM_L. This difference, if significant, may imply that the profit margins of FCEs are higher than those of their local counterparts, even after taking into account the influence of market structural factors. The individual explanatory variables included in these equations also affect PCM_F and PCM_L differently. In what follows we discuss the performance of these explanatory variables in explaining variation in the dependent variables.

The coefficients of advertising intensity variables ADS and ADCON were not significant. ADCON is highly collinear with $SKIL_1$ and $SKIL_2$. To check whether its poor performance was due to multicollinearity, $SKIL_1$ and $SKIL_2$ were dropped from one set of equations. In the absence of skill variables ADCON was significant at the 5 per cent level in the case of PCM_F, and at the 15 per cent level in the case of PCM_L. However, the exclusion of SKIL drastically affects the R^{-2} as well as the performance of other variables in the PCM_F equation. On the other hand, exclusion of ADS and ADCON has only a marginal (0.1 per cent) effect on the proportion of variation explained by the PCM_F equation. This suggests that in the absence of SKIL, ADCON picks up its influence. Its own contribution to the variation appears to be insignificant. One possible explanation for this finding can be that in a country like India—where government policy has restricted both internal as well as external competition and where firms, particularly up to 1980 (which in fact is our reference period), enjoyed a seller's market—advertising might not have the role in influencing profit margins that it has in more competitive settings in industrialized countries. It might also indicate the viability of non-advertising–intensive strategies that has been found in Canada's case by Caves and Pugel (1980). Also, the measurement of advertising intensity may have limitations in reflecting the economies of scale in advertising as noted by Comanor and Wilson (1974), and the capitalized value of past advertisement expenditures.

TECH, a proxy for the intensity of industry in technological inputs, as well as $SKIL_1$ and $SKIL_2$, the alternative proxies for the industry's intensity in human skills, are consistently significant with a positive sign in explaining variation in PCM_F. In PCM_L equations, however, they have a negative sign and are not significant. This finding suggests that skill and technology intensity entry barriers protect FCEs from the competition of both new entrants and existing local firms. The knowledge-intensive industries are usually producer goods industries. Market transactions of products of these industries are influenced not only by the technical specification of the individual product concerned, but also by other factors, such as width of the product range offered by the particular supplier, his reputation and overall technological strength. FCEs represent their respective global enterprises and their technological competence and experience all over the world.

Most MNE affiliates in India, particularly in the early post-Independence period, were set up in response to the import-substitution drive (Davies 1977). They might have served the Indian market through exports before starting local production. Hence, many of the FCEs may have inherited a built-up clientele and goodwill. In comparison, local firms in the business, offering equally good products based on technology obtained through licensing or their own R&D, suffer from several disadvantages. They do not enjoy ready market acceptance and must develop markets from scratch. Being new to business the range of products and associated services offered by them is unlikely to be as wide as that of FCEs. It appears, therefore, that FCEs and LCEs serve different market segments. FCEs serve the top end of the respective markets, which consists of discriminating buyers who accept higher prices, whereas LCEs concentrate on the lower end of the market. The above advantage enjoyed by FCEs over LCEs varies with knowledge intensity of the industry.

The absolute capital requirement entry barrier (AKR) is insignificant, with a positive sign in the case of PCM_F. It is not significant even in the absence of $SIZE_F$ with which it is highly collinear. This entry barrier, therefore, does not particularly protect FCEs. AKR is, however, consistently significant, with a negative sign, in explaining PCM_L. It suggests that local firms suffer from a disadvantage in high capital requiring industries. Usually capital-intensive industries are expected to be more profitable. This finding, therefore, is startling. The availability of capital may not be such a big barrier in the Indian case because of well-developed capital markets and public financial institutions. But the industrial licensing policy of the government regulates entry into large capital requiring industries. The inverse relationship between AKR and PCM_L could be due to the rampant underutilization of capacities which characterizes Indian industries.[2] The loss of surplus on account of underutilization of capital would be higher in large capital-requiring industries because of greater fixed costs (capital equipment). But if this explanation of the inverse relationship between PCM_L and AKR is valid, then the insignificance of such relationship in the case of PCM_F may imply that FCEs tend to have better capacity utilization than their local counterparts. However, more work on the nature of this relationship is needed before a definite conclusion can be reached.

The length of the production process or vertical integration proxy, VAS, has a positive and significant coefficient explaining variation in both PCM_F and PCM_L. It suggests that the length of the production process is a source of an industry-specific entry barrier. The length of the production process gives an edge to existing firms over their potential rivals, and hence, deters entry. Thus, it has a favourable effect on profit margins of all existing firms—foreign controlled or local.

The firm size variable is significant in both cases, PCM_F as well as PCM_L, but with different signs. For profit margins of FCEs it has a negative sign, and a positive sign in the case of PCM_L. This result has to be interpreted in the light of the findings of chapter 4 regarding firm size. FCEs have on average been found to be of a considerably larger size than their local counterparts. The relationship between firm size and profitability has been hypothesized to be an inverted U-shape, that is profitability rises with size to a certain extent and declines afterwards when X-inefficiencies start operating. It appears that FCEs are in the latter half of the inverted U because of their larger size, while local firms are still in the first half.[3] Previous studies, like those of Singh and Whittington (1968), and Shepherd (1972), have reported a negative size–profitability relationship for larger firms. Connor and Mueller (1982) have also found a negative relationship in the case of affiliates of US MNEs in Mexico and Brazil. More detailed work at the firm level is needed before a more definitive statement on the nature of the relationship between firm size and profitability can be made.

Tests of Significance of Heterogeneity of Profit Functions

To examine the statistical significance of dissimilarities of intercepts and slopes of profit functions of FCEs and LCEs, we made use of co-variance analysis. This procedure involves contrasting (in terms of an F-test) the residual sums of squares in a restricted model in which hypothetical equality is imposed, to those of the unrestricted models where intercepts and slopes are allowed to vary across FCEs and LCEs (see Johnston 1972, ch. 6 for details). In addition to unrestricted profit functions of FCEs and LCEs, (see Table 5.2) we needed to fit restricted profit functions. The following two profit functions (corresponding to equations (*1*) and (*3*) in Table 5.2) were fitted on 86 observations pooled across FCEs and LCEs. Equation 5.6 makes the restrictive assumption of complete similarity of the profit functions of FCEs and LCEs.

$$PCM_i = \alpha_0 + \beta_1 ADS + \beta_2 ADCON + \beta_3 TECH + \beta_4 SKIL_2 + \beta_5 AKR + \beta_6 VAS + \beta_7 SIZE_i \quad (5.6)$$

Equation (5.7) allows intercepts of the two groups to vary by introducing an intercept dummy variable (DFOR) taking a value of one for FCEs and zero otherwise:

$$PCM_i = \alpha_0 + \beta_0 DFOR + \beta_1 ADS + \beta_2 ADCON + \beta_3 TECH + \beta_4 SKIL_2 + \beta_5 AKR + \beta_6 VAS + \beta_7 SIZE_i \quad (5.7)$$

The estimated versions of these equations are as follows:

Restricted profit functions:

$$PCM_i = \underset{}{2.489} - \underset{(-.727)}{.0902\,ADS} + \underset{(2.177)}{1.523\,ADCON} + \underset{(1.280)}{.060\,TECH} - \underset{(.685)}{.463\,SKIL_2} - \underset{(2.357)}{.824\,AKR} + \underset{(1.848)}{1.937\,VAS} + \underset{(4.357)}{1.220\,SIZE_i} \quad (5.6)$$

$R^{-2} = .276 \quad F = 4.257$

sum of squared residuals = 269.78 N = 86

$$PCM_i = 2.177 + \underset{(1.762)}{.784\,DFOR} - \underset{(.680)}{.076\,ADS} + \underset{(2.094)}{1.448\,ADCON} + \underset{(1.313)}{.061\,TECH} - \underset{(.680)}{.454\,SKIL_2} - \underset{(1.705)}{.620\,AKR} + \underset{(1.711)}{1.775\,VAS} + \underset{(3.121)}{.970\,SIZE_i} \quad (5.7)$$

R^{-2} = .304 F = 4.213
sum of squared residuals = 259.330 N = 86

(Figures in parenthesis are t-values).

Table 5.3

Test of Heterogeneity of Profit Functions

Model	*Sum of squared residuals*	*Degrees of freedom (d.f.)*	*Mean squares*	*F-test (d.f.)*
Restricted (equation 5.6)	S_0 = 269.78	78	3.46	
Partially restricted (equation 5.7)	S_1 = 259.33 Incremental (differential intercepts) $S_2 = S_0 - S_1$ = 10.45	77 1	3.37 10.45	Test of differential intercepts: F_1 = 3.10 (1,77)
Unrestricted (equations (1) and (3) in Table 5.2)	S_3 = 5.79 + 177.61=183.40 Incremental (differential slope vectors) $S_4 = S_1 - S_3$ = 75.93	70 7	2.62 10.85	Test of differential slope vectors: F_2 = 4.14* (7,70)
	Total incremental $S_5 = S_2 + S_4$ = 85.38	7	12.10	Test of overall heterogeneity: F_3 = 4.71* (7,70)

* Indicates significant at one per cent level.

The FCE dummy DFOR has a positive coefficient which is statistically significant at the 10 per cent level in terms of the t-test. Table 5.4 summarizes the co-variance analysis based on equations *(1)* and *(3)* of Table 5.2 and Equations (5.6) and (5.7). The F-tests conducted on residuals in restricted and unrestricted models suggest that differences in the intercepts of profit functions of FCEs and LCEs are not statistically significant (F_1). Differences in the slope vectors as well as the overall profit functions, however, are significant at the 1 per cent level of confidence (F_2 and F_3). This finding, therefore, tends to rule out the possibility of inter-group ability differences as the source of superior profit margins of FCEs. The differential slope vectors uphold the proposition that FCEs and LCEs in Indian manufacturing constitute different strategic groups and enjoy differential protection from mobility barriers.[4]

Conclusions

This chapter examined the determinants of profit margins of FCEs and LCEs in 43 Indian manufacturing industries to seek explanations for the superior performance of the former. A set of hypotheses pertaining to the likely determinants were formulated. Two theoretical possibilities were considered for explaining superior profit margins of FCEs. Profit margins of FCEs might be higher because of their superior ability or FCEs and LCEs may constitute different strategic groups and entry barriers may protect them differently.

The empirical analysis finds support for the proposition that FCEs and LCEs belong to different strategic groups in an industry and that the former are more protected by entry barriers than their local counterparts. In knowledge-intensive industries (that is, intensive in both technology and human skills), FCEs appear to enjoy special advantages over their local counterparts. This is because in these industries the overall technological strength and reputation of an enterprise, and width of product range and associated services, play a crucial role in market transactions. Being part of global enterprises, FCEs enjoy a formidable edge over LCEs in all these respects. The two groups of firms, therefore, appear to be serving different market segments: FCEs capturing the upper end of the market (which accepts high prices) and LCEs concentrating on the lower end. A part of the higher profit margins of FCEs might be on account of their greater degree of vertical integration (observed in chapter 4), and possibly their better utilization of capital. Inter-group ability differences, if they exist at all, do not appear to be significant in explaining profitability differences.

The degree of seller concentration and protection from imports accorded to local industry are not found to be related to profitability in India's case. Perhaps operational inefficiency resulting from the lack of competition nullifies the favourable effect which these two factors might have had on profitability.

In Indian manufacturing industries, advertising intensity does not appear to play the role that it does in more competitive settings. This could also be due to measurement problems and the viability of non-advertisement intensive strategies.

Notes

1. This, however, necessitated adding trivial values to a few observations having zero or negative values.
2. See Corporate Studies Group (1983) for recent evidence on the under-utilization of capacity.
3. Since these relationships have been estimated separately for FCEs and LCEs, the possible non-linearity could not be captured through a squared term.
4. The co-variance analysis presented above indicates the statistical significance of the overall slope vectors of the profit functions of FCEs and LCEs. Which of the individual regression coefficients are significantly different is not clear from this analysis. The only way of finding out is to fit additional models with slope dummy variables capturing differential slopes for individual variables. Such an analysis was also attempted by us. However, due to severe multicollinearity among different dummy variables it landed us in the dummy variable trap. Hence, it proved to be futile.

6

Export Behaviour of Foreign and Local Enterprises in Indian Manufacturing

Introduction

FCEs are generally considered to be better placed to tap international markets than their local counterparts in view of their captive access to the information and marketing networks of their parent enterprises (de la Torre 1974). The Indian government gave due recognition to this contention and extended additional incentives to induce FCEs to export a greater proportion of their output from India. In a significant proportion of cases, export obligations were also imposed at the time of entry or expansion. These factors led one to expect that the export performance of FCEs would be better than that of their local counterparts. But the empirical analysis in chapter 4 did not reveal any statistically significant difference between (average or weighted) export performance of FCEs and LCEs in 43 Indian manufacturing industries.

The analysis of Chapter 4, however, focused on the overall statistical significance of the differences in export performance. Their differential advantages may cause the industry composition of exports of FCEs and LCEs to be different. It is possible that FCEs export those products which would not have been exported in their absence. An examination of the determinants of exports of FCEs and LCEs may, therefore, facilitate an understanding of their relative roles in promoting India's manufactured exports. This chapter examines the determinants of export performance of FCEs and LCEs in 43 Indian industries. It formulates hypotheses concerning the determinants of export performance, presents empirical results, and comments on the main findings.

Determinants of Export Performance: Hypotheses

The inter-industry variation in export performance of FCEs and LCEs (respectively EXP_F and EXP_L) can be analysed in terms of industry and firm characteristics in the framework of the neo-factor endowments and neo-technology theories of international trade which are complementary (Hughes 1986). Some of these possible determinants of export performance are:

Industry Characteristics

Capital Intensity

According to the Heckscher-Ohlin theorem, labour surplus developing countries like India are not likely to enjoy any advantage in exporting capital-intensive goods. This general disadvantage in exports of capital-intensive goods may be equally applicable to both FCEs and LCEs. Even theories of the new international division of labour predict that MNEs export labour-intensive, and not capital-intensive, products from developing countries (Kojima 1978). Hence, we shall expect the export performance of both groups of firms to be inversely related to the capital intensity of the industry. In view of the lack of data on physical labour employed, the capital intensity will be proxied by capital-output ratio (COR).

COR Total capital employed as a proportion of net industry sales, averaged over three years: 1978–79 to 1980–81.

Skill Intensity

India possesses one of the largest pools of scientific and technical manpower in the world. Neo-factor endowment theories of trade (Johnson 1970) might, therefore, expect India to enjoy a comparative advantage in export of skill-intensive goods. This, however, does not appear to be the case. The skill-intensive industries in India in general are not mature enough to be internationally competitive. In an analysis of the characteristics of skill-intensive industries, Hirsch (1970) has brought out the sources of disadvantages which a developing country would suffer in exporting these products. Price competitiveness is not a major factor in the exports of high skill-intensive products because of their relatively inelastic demand. Instead, the marketing organization, and 'proprietary associations abroad' are of critical significance for exports of these products. In the present context FCEs enjoy benefits of proprietary associations abroad as their parent and associate companies are located in different parts of the world. Hence, FCEs should find it easier to export skill-intensive products than their local counterparts. Therefore, the export performance of FCEs can be expected to be positively related to skill intensity. The export performance of local firms may be inversely related to the index of skill intensity, which reflects the disadvantage they face in these industries. The skill intensity of an industry will be captured through two alternative proxies, namely, $SKIL_1$ and $SKIL_2$, as in the previous chapters.

- $SKIL_1$ Non-production workers as a proportion of the total work-force in 1978–79.
- $SKIL_2$ Earnings of high salaried employees (those receiving Rs 3,000 per month or more) as a proportion of total salaries and wage bill, averaged over three years: 1978–79 to 1980–81.

Technology Intensity

Neo-technology theories of international trade emphasize the role of the technology gap in determining a country's international trade pattern (Posner 1961; Vernon 1966; Hufbauer 1966). Gruber, Mehta, and Vernon (1967), and Gruber and Vernon (1970), have found the 'technology factor' to be important in international trade and have observed that industries associated with a relatively high 'research effort' also tend to export a relatively high proportion of their output. The United States is a prime example. Hughes (1986) noted the role of the neo-technology theories in explaining exports of the United Kingdom and other developed countries.[1] Developing countries like India are, however, borrowers of technology unlike the United States. The bulk of whatever little in-house R&D is undertaken in India is spent on adapting imported technology rather than on new developments (Desai 1980). Therefore, they are likely to be in an apparently disadvantageous position in the export of technology-intensive goods. Hence, an industry's intensity in the use of technological inputs can be expected to be inversely related to its export performance. Dasgupta and Siddharthan (1985) have found Indian exports to consist largely of standardized goods with a low skill and technological content. The general disadvantage of the developing country firms in technology-intensive industries, however, may not apply to FCEs which are supposed to have continuous access to R&D laboratories of their parent and associate companies. Therefore, while expecting a negative relationship between technology intensity and export performance of local firms, a possibility of a positive relationship between technology intensity and export performance of FCEs exists.

The measurement of technology intensity (TECH) of an industry will take into account both imported and local sources of technology, as in chapter 5.

TECH In-house R&D expenditure and remittances on account of royalty and technical fees as a proportion of net sales, averaged over three years: 1978–79 to 1980–81.

Product Differentiation

India, like other developing countries, is at a disadvantage in the export of goods characterized by product differentiation through brand or trade names, and those in which advertising and sales promotion plays an important role. FCEs with their access to brand names and marketing channels of their parent MNEs can overcome the handicaps faced by developing country firms. We shall, therefore, expect an inverse relationship between EXP_L and advertising intensity (ADS), and a positive relationship between EXP_F and ADS.

ADS Advertising expenditure as a proportion of net industry sales, averaged over three years: 1978–79 to 1980–81.

Degree of Local and Foreign Competition

In an activity like exporting, price competitiveness is of crucial importance. Therefore, efficiency should be positively related to export performance. Panchamukhi (1978, ch. 8), in an empirical study of Indian firms, found the efficiency parameter to be important for firms to distinguish themselves as exporters. Operational efficiency is related to the degree of competition. We consider two aspects of competition: the degree of seller competition and the extent of protection from external competition; the former is proxied by the four-firm concentration ratio (CR4), and the latter by effective rates of protection (ERPs). Both these proxies are inversely related to the degree of competition, and hence, are expected to be negatively related to export performance.

CR4 Share of top four firms in net industry sales, averaged over three years: 1978–79 to 1980–81.

ERP Effective rates of protection, for 1979–80, Cordon method; as estimated by NCAER.

Firm Characteristics

Successful export efforts involve considerable investment in market development, building-up an image abroad, etc. These activities may have certain minimum threshold levels for being effective. There might be a minimum sales volume, which must be reached before exporting becomes possible (Hirsch and Bijaoui 1985). Exporting involves significant economies of scale in setting up a marketing network abroad, in gathering market information, etc. (Caves *et al.* 1980). Further, exporting is associated with a high degree of uncertainty and risk. Therefore, large and profitable firms can be expected to be better equipped to venture into international markets. Hence, we expect firm size ($SIZE_i$) and profitability (PCM_i) to be positively related with export performance. Some studies have postulated an influence of export-orientation on profitability. Such a relationship in the present case, however, is unlikely because exports account for only about 5 per cent of the sample firm's output.

$SIZE_i$ Average net sales per firm in group i in 1980–81 (i=FCE, LCE).

PCM_i Profits before taxes of ith group of firms as a proportion of their net worth in 1980–81 (i=FCE, LCE).

To sum up, the export performance of FCEs and LCEs is postulated to be influenced by different industry and firm characteristics as follows:

$$EXP_F = f_1\,(\underset{-}{COR},\ \underset{+}{SKIL},\ \underset{+}{TECH},\ \underset{+}{ADS},\ \underset{-}{CR4},\ \underset{-}{ERP},\ \underset{+}{PCM_F},\ \underset{+}{SIZE_F}) \qquad (6.1)$$

$$EXP_L = f_2\,(\underset{-}{COR},\ \underset{-}{SKIL},\ \underset{-}{TECH},\ \underset{-}{ADS},\ \underset{-}{CR4},\ \underset{-}{ERP},\ \underset{+}{PCM_L},\ \underset{+}{SIZE_L}) \qquad (6.2)$$

Signs indicate the nature of relationship. The measurement of the dependent variable is as follows:

EXP_i Exports as a proportion of net sales for ith group of firms in 1980–81 (i=FCEs, LCEs).

Empirical Analysis

Equations 6.1 and 6.2 were fitted for the data for 43 Indian manufacturing industries. All the variables were transformed into logarithms to reduce possible heteroskedasticity. Table 6.1 presents select regression equations. CR4 and ERP were not significant in any equation, hence, they were dropped from the equations. These variables were also not significant in explaining export performance of Canadian industries (Caves *et al.* 1980).

The variables included in the equations explain a rather small proportion of the variation in the dependent variable as reflected by poor values of R^{-2} (though significant in the F-test). This, however, is not a case peculiar to Indian data.

Similar export functions estimated for the United Kingdom also had poor R^{-2} (Hughes 1986).

Table 6.1
Regression Equations Explaining Export Performance of FCEs and LCEs in Indian Manufacturing

Independent variables	*Dependent variable*			
	EXP_F		*EXP_L*	
	1	*2*	*3*	*4*
1. COR	−2.333[c] (1.733)	−2.118 (1.468)	−.621 (.592)	−.314 (.293)
2. $SKIL_1$	−2.521[c] (1.901)		−1.487 (1.470)	
3. $SKIL_2$		−.189 (.155)		−1.088 (1.399)
4. TECH	.112 (1.368)	.094 (1.091)	−.070 (1.083)	−.064 (.974)
5. ADS	−.107 (.484)	−.113 (.475)	.305[c] (1.699)	.334[c] (1.833)
6. $SIZE_i$	1.068[a] (2.995)	.884[b] (2.09)	−.340 (.969)	−.327 (.950)
7. PCM_i	1.642[b] (2.100)	1.143 (1.333)	.349[a] (3.140)	.319[a] (2.879)
3. Intercept	−8.45	−13.719	2.554	.279
R^{-2}	.323	.256	.354	.351
F	2.868	2.064	3.294	3.245
N	43	43	43	43

Note: Figures in parentheses are t-values. Superscript letters indicate levels of significance as follows: (*a*) 1%; (*b*) 5%; (*c*) 10%; (2-tailed test).

Among industry characteristics, the capital intensity variable COR has the expected negative sign throughout. In the case of FCEs it is significant at the 10 per cent level and is not significant for LCEs. This finding confirms the hypothesis that India does not have an advantage in capital-intensive industries. The alternative proxies of skill intensity are with a negative sign throughout and, except for $SKIL_1$ in the case of FCEs (which is significant at 10 per cent level), they are not significant. Thus, Indian firms appear to be at a disadvantage in skill-intensive industries. Lall and Mohammad (1983b) also found a similar performance of this variable in explaining Indian exports. The coefficient of TECH is with a positive sign in the case of FCEs and a negative sign in the case of LCEs, but is not significant. Thus, the 'technology factor' is not important for Indian manufactured exports.

The product differentiation variable, ADS, is insignificant in the case of FCEs with a negative sign but is significant (though only at 10 per cent) with a positive sign in explaining the export performance of local firms. FCEs, therefore, do not export differentiated goods from India. The positive and significant coefficient in the case of local firms seems to be on account of exports of a wide range of consumer goods to East European countries under the rupee trade agreement. In these markets, lack of established brand/trade names is not a big handicap.

Among the firm characteristics, average firm size has a positive and significant relationship with the export performance of FCEs. But it is insignificant, with a negative sign, in the case of local firms. A similar negative and insignificant relationship between size and export rate has been observed by M.S. Kumar (1984, ch. 8) in the case of the United Kingdom. It implies that smaller local firms appear to be at least as dynamic in exports as larger ones. Here again, easy access of small local manufacturers of consumer goods to East European markets might explain the insignificance of the size factor in the case of local firms. In the case of FCEs, however, size significantly determines their export performance. It can therefore, be inferred that the rupee trade agreement between India and the East European countries has helped the former export products that are very unlikely to have been exported in its absence, namely, brand sensitive consumer goods from smaller local firms. Profitability has the expected positive sign throughout and is significant (except in equation (2), perhaps because of its collinearity with $SKIL_2$). It upholds the expectation that profitable firms (both foreign and local) are more likely to venture into international markets.

The above findings, therefore, do not reveal any major differences in the role of industry characteristics in explaining the export performance of FCEs and LCEs. Except in the case of ADS, which is significant in explaining export performance of local firms, they are all insignificant for both FCEs and LCEs. This suggests that FCEs and LCEs do not export products with different industry characteristics. Alternatively, the industry composition of exports of the two groups of firms is not very different.

FCEs and Exports: A Comment

The empirical analysis of chapter 4, and the present chapter, does not bring out any statistically significant differences in either export performance or industry characteristics of exports of FCEs and their local counterparts in Indian manufacturing. These findings are in line with those of earlier studies for India and other developing countries. For Latin American countries, Morgenstern and Mueller (1976), Newfarmer and Marsh (1981), and Fairchild and Sosin (1986) also did not find any significant differences between export performance of FCEs and LCEs. Subrahmanian and Pillai (1979) for India, Jenkins (1979) for Mexico, and Kirim (1986) for the Turkish pharmaceutical industry found export performance of FCEs to be inferior to that of their local counterparts.

It appears, therefore, that affiliates of MNEs set up in response to the import substitution drive are confined largely to the domestic market. The attempts of the host government to induce them to export a higher proportion of output have had only limited success. The industrialization and trade policies that were pursued in the broad framework of import substitution led, in general, to sheltered markets and high costs. Such an environment in an economy with a large and expanding home market made an inward-oriented market strategy a far more attractive option for firms than venturing abroad. This has applied to both FCEs and LCEs. In recent years the Indian government has taken steps to liberalize the economy and expose local industry to competition in order to promote international competitiveness. An examination of the response of FCEs and LCEs to these policies, however, has to await more up-to-date data.

Notes

1. Cheng (1984) provides a review of additional evidence.

7

Summary and Conclusions

This study examined the industrial distribution, characteristics, and performance of FCEs in the Indian manufacturing sector. The specific objectives of the study were: (*a*) to compute shares of FCEs in overall and individual manufacturing industries; (*b*) to analyse the determinants of inter-industry variation in foreign shares; (*c*) to examine the discriminating characteristics of FCEs and LCEs; (*d*) to analyse the determinants of profit margins of FCEs and LCEs; and (*e*) to analyse the relative export behaviour of FCEs. This chapter summarizes the major findings of the study, their implications, and limitations.

FCEs, as defined in the study, are Indian affiliates of Western MNEs. They share the ownership of intangible assets with the parent MNEs, such as brand names and goodwill, proprietary technology, organizational and technical skills, captive access to information, and marketing networks. The ownership of these intangible assets provides a conceptual connecting link to the seemingly diverse aspects of FCEs considered in the study. Ownership advantages enjoy a central place in the theory of international operations of the firm (see the works of Hymer, Kindleberger, Caves, Dunning, Buckley and Casson, Rugman, and Teece) that has been used to explain inter-industry differences in foreign shares. These ownership advantages may also explain the differences in conduct and performance of FCEs and their local counterparts. The asset bundles of FCEs and LCEs are different because of the ownership advantages of the former. Besides, being part of an MNE, certain decisions of FCEs are subject to centralized decision-making which responds to global opportunities. These factors might lead to strategic differences between the two groups of firms, which are reflected in turn in a number of parameters of conduct and performance. If there are strategic differences between FCEs and LCEs, entry barriers may not protect them equally and hence, their profit margins may differ. Ownership advantages also give FCEs an edge over their local counterparts in export markets, particularly in differentiated, and skill and technology-intensive products. This may lead to possible differences in their export behaviour.

The study had to overcome severe gaps in the data availability on the operations of FCEs. To circumvent these difficulties two exclusive variable sets for 54 manufacturing industries were created with the help of unpublished financial statistics of 1,334 medium and large, non-government public limited manufacturing companies collected by the RBI. These variable sets put together a large number of structural and behavioural variables, hitherto not available at such a level of disaggregation.

The Policy Framework

The Indian government's attitude towards foreign investments has varied during the post-Independence period. There was a gradual liberalization of policy in the early post-Independence period (up to 1967). Between the late 1960s and the late 1970s regulatory and screening procedures were streamlined, and the policy was made relatively stricter. During the 1980s the policy was again liberalized. In the 1990s the policy has been made more open and transparent as a part of the structural adjustment programme undertaken by the government. Automatic permission is now accorded to foreign investment proposals in 35 priority industries with up to to 51 percent foreign equity if they bring in enough foreign exchange to cover capital goods imports.

The selective policy has influenced the pattern of FDI in

a number of ways. First, most of the FDI during the post-Independence period was directed towards the manufacturing sector. The share of manufacturing in total FDI stock increased from 40 per cent in 1964 to nearly 85 per cent by 1990. This proportion is higher than that in the overall flows of FDI to all developing countries. Within the manufacturing sector the share of modern and technology-intensive sectors, such as electrical goods, non-electrical machinery and machine tools, chemicals, and medicines and pharmaceuticals, has gone up compared to traditional sectors, such as food and beverages, textile products, and toiletries and other chemical products. Second, most (98 per cent in 1990) FDI is now subject to Indian corporate legislation (as against 54 per cent in 1964). Furthermore, there is evidence of a wider acceptance by MNEs of minority ownership as a mode of FDI. Finally, there has been a diversification of the sources of FDI; while the share of the United Kingdom has gone down from nearly 77 per cent in 1964 to 49 per cent in 1990, that of the United States has gone up from 14.5 per cent to 19 per cent during the same period. Germany, Switzerland and Japan have emerged as other important sources of FDI in India.

Share of FCEs in the Manufacturing Sector

Previous estimates of the share of FCEs in sales or assets of the organized private corporate sector have ranged from 25 to 50 per cent, depending upon the sample used and the reference period. In this study the share of FCEs in sales or assets of large private corporate sector was estimated to be around 23 per cent in 1980–81 (depending upon the coverage of sample). Their share in profits was much higher than in either sales or assets. Inter-temporal comparisons indicated a decline in foreign shares over the period from 1972–73 to 1980–81. This suggested the reversal of the trend of an increasing share of FCEs noted by previous studies for an earlier period. This perhaps was an outcome of the particularly restrictive policy followed by the government towards foreign investments during the seventies when some nationalizations and disinvestments also took place. FCEs, however, continued to be constituents of a significant and more prosperous segment of the private corporate sector.

The shares of FCEs in sales of 54 branches (three-digit) of manufacturing were also computed in the large private corporate sector. These were found to vary widely across industries. Of the 54 sectors, FCEs accounted for more than two-thirds of sample sales in 11 industries, between one-third and two-thirds in 15 industries, and had a significant presence in nine industries with shares below one-third. In 12 industries, FCEs were of marginal consequence and they did not exist in seven. Compared to the sixties for which some information is available, these sectoral shares have undergone considerable change as a consequence of the government's policy of containing market power of FCEs by encouraging local firms. Foreign shares have completely disappeared from a number of traditional industries such as jute and cotton textiles, paper, cement, and sugar. In consumer goods industries characterized by product differentiation, such as processed foods, cigarettes, leather products, dry batteries, medicines, toiletries, however, foreign shares have continued to be high despite the government's policy in this regard and the relative simplicity of the technology involved. This can be attributed to brand loyalties enjoyed by the firms, as well as other entry barriers.

Determinants of Industrial Distribution of Foreign Shares

The recent extensions of the theory of internationalization of the firm predict the incidence of FDI (and hence foreign shares) to be high in those branches of industry in which intangible assets characterized by locational and high internalization incentives provide a competitive edge to firms. Licensing is expected to be preferred when internalization incentives are low.

Empirical tests of these predictions have, however, been constrained mainly by the difficulty in actually classifying intangible assets between those with high and low internalization incentives. This study assessed the nature of four broad categories of intangible assets: product differentiation and goodwill, knowledge embodied in human skills (idiosyncracies) or tacit knowledge, knowledge embodied in capital goods, and access to sources of capital. The first two were judged to have high, and the latter two low, internalization incentives. Variables proxying each of these intangible assets as well as policy induced locational factors, such as import substitution, protection, entry regulations, and industrial policy, were constructed. The empirical test involved regressing foreign shares and intensity of licensing on all these variables across 49 manufacturing industries.

The findings suggested that foreign shares were high in those branches of manufacturing that were characterized by a high degree of product differentiation; hence brand goodwill could be a formidable competitive advantage. They were also high in industries intensive in the use of knowledge embodied in human skills. On the other hand, licensing was a dominant mode of foreign operation in industries intensive in the use of knowledge embodied in capital goods. The access to sources of capital was unimportant for both FDI and licensing. This could be due to the development of the capital markets and the presence of public financial institutions in the country. Licensing, and not FDI, dominated the industries which exhibited some local R&D activity. But this might be due to the fact that R&D in India is mainly of an adaptive nature and has been undertaken in areas using less complex technology. The import substitution programme of the government encouraged the erstwhile exporters to the country to set up local production facilities. The government's selective policy appears to have discouraged both FDI and licensing in the consumer goods sectors where local skills were available in some measure.

Discriminating Characteristics of FCEs

Comparisons of the conduct and performance of FCEs and LCEs can be helpful in evaluating the effects of FCEs on the host economy. Previous studies comparing the characteristics of FCEs and LCEs by and large had small samples, and were conducted in an univariate context. Besides, a number of important aspects relating to the conduct of firms were not analysed.

This exercise considered 15 parameters for purposes of comparison, denoting such diverse characteristics as the scale of operations, advertising and R&D intensities, profitability and growth, choice of technology, employee compensation and skills, magnitude of vertical local linkages, export performance, and various aspects of financial strategy and management. Predictions on the nature of differences between FCEs and LCEs were made on the basis of general attributes of MNEs and existing evidence from India and abroad. The exercise was conducted for a sample of 49 Indian manufacturing industries and the statistical significance of the differences was evaluated using appropriate statistical tools in both univariate and multivariate frameworks.

The statistical findings suggest that FCEs have larger scales of operation and enjoy higher profit margins than their local counterparts. The proportion of sales spent on advertising by FCEs is not significantly different from that of LCEs but the efficiency of advertising by FCEs may be higher because of economies of scale and internalization of a part of goodwill generated by the advertising done by their associate companies the world over. R&D intensity and growth rates of FCEs are found to be lower only on account of extraneous influences. Factor proportions do not appear to be significantly different between the groups, but caution needs to be exercised while interpreting this finding because of limitations of measurement. A higher proportions of FCE employees are in the high income category than their local counterparts, on account of their tendency to employ qualitatively superior personnel by offering higher emoluments. In the case of skill-intensive industries, this could be an aspect of non-price rivalry and a source of a contrived entry barrier.

FCEs tend to have a greater degree of vertical integration than LCEs. Hence, they generate fewer vertical inter-firm linkages with the host economy than their local counterparts. The degree of import dependence of FCEs is not significantly different from that of local firms. FCEs also do not export a significantly different proportion of sales than their local counterparts.

The behaviour of FCEs in terms of retention ratios, dependence on borrowed funds, and tax planning is different only on account of extraneous influences. Their respective inventory management practices are also not very different from each other. FCEs, however, enjoy a more comfortable liquidity position due to superior access to long-term sources of financing of their working capital.

The picture of FCEs that emerges from the analysis, therefore, is one of relatively large, more prosperous, vertically integrated, fund-rich firms with better paid personnel. Some industry variation, however, does exist. In some industries, such as motor vehicles, machine tools, man-made fibres, asbestos and asbestos cement, and automobile tyres and tubes, local firms affiliated to large local industrial houses with the complement of technology obtained on licence from abroad have closely resembled their foreign controlled counterparts in almost all the dimensions covered.

Profit Behaviour

To seek an explanation for the higher profit margins of FCEs, determinants of profitability of FCEs and LCEs were analysed. In view of recent theoretical propositions, inter-group profitability differences could exist if FCEs and LCEs constituted different strategic groups within an industry and enjoyed differential protection from entry barriers. They could also be due to possible inter-group ability differences. To explore these propositions the profit functions of FCEs and LCEs were estimated across 43 manufacturing industries using variables representing different sources of entry barriers, firm size, degree of seller concentration, growth rate, and levels of effective protection as the main determinants. In addition to the standard sources of entry barriers—product differentiation, skill intensity, and absolute capital requirements—two other sources—the intensity of industry in the use of technological inputs, and the length of production runs (degree of vertical integration)—were also considered.

The empirical results offer support for the proposition that FCEs and LCEs belong to different strategic groups in an industry and that FCEs are protected by entry barriers more than their local counterparts. The profit margins of FCEs (and not of LCEs) are found to be significantly related to industry's intensity in the use of technological and skill inputs. FCEs, therefore, appear to enjoy special advantages over their local counterparts in knowledge-intensive industries (that is, intensive both in process and product technology, and human skills). This is because in such industries the overall technological strength and reputation of an enterprise, the width of the product and range of services play a crucial role in market transactions. Being part of global enterprises, FCEs enjoy a formidable edge over LCEs in these respects. It is possible that the two groups of firms serve different market segments; FCEs concentrating on the upper end of the market, consisting of discriminating consumers who can accept higher prices, and LCEs concentrating on the usually more price-competitive lower end. Part of the higher profits might be on account of their greater degree of vertical integration.

The degree of seller concentration and protection from imports for the local industry are not found to be related to profitability in India's case. One of the reasons could be that operational inefficiency resulting from the lack of competition nullifies the possible favourable effect. Advertising intensity in Indian manufacturing also does not appear to play the role that it does in more competitive settings. This could, perhaps, be due to the viability of non-advertising intensive strategies.

Export Behaviour

The export behaviour of FCEs and LCEs was further analysed to bring out the differences, if any, in the industry characteristics of the exports of FCEs and LCEs. The export functions were fitted for Indian manufacturing industries in the framework of the neo-factor endowments and the neo-technology theories of international trade. The empirical results did not reveal any significant difference in the industry characteristics of exports of FCEs and LCEs. Hence, the industry composition of exports of FCEs and LCEs is not significantly different. Firm size appeared to be an important determinant of exports only for FCEs. Therefore, while only larger FCEs concentrate on exports, smaller LCEs appear to be as dynamic as larger ones in this respect. The significant positive relationship observed between advertising intensity and export performance of LCEs is partly on account of their exports of consumer goods to East European countries under the rupee trade agreement. In these markets lack of established brand and trade names does not imply a big handicap. Firm profitability turns out to be a significant determinant of export performance in both cases.

Thus, this study does not reveal any statistically significant difference in either export performance or industry characteristics of exports of FCEs and their local counterparts in Indian manufacturing. In view of their captive access to the information and marketing networks of their parents, affiliates of MNEs are generally considered to be better placed to tap international markets than their local counterparts. However, the decision to export from the host country, being an important aspect of the global strategy of the enterprise, is not taken on the basis of advantages alone. In a large economy with a sheltered and growing home market, such as India, an inward-oriented marketing strategy appeared a far more attractive option for MNEs than using it as an export platform. Hence, they seem to have opted for it in the same way as their local counterparts.

Implications of the Findings, Policy Applications, and Directions for Further Work

The above findings have certain implications for the economic analysis of the theories of industrial organization and international operations of the firm. For instance, the analysis of the determinants of inter-industry variations in the intensity of FDI and licensing, by and large, upholds the role of internalization incentives in influencing the choice of the mode of foreign expansion. Dunning (1984), Contractor (1984), and Davidson and McFetridge (1984, 1985) have analysed the factors influencing the proportion of internal (external) transactions in total flows of technology through inter-country studies. The present study further extends the analysis by undertaking a rigorous test of recent propositions in the inter-industry context.

Second, the findings of the analysis of discriminating characteristics of foreign controlled and local firms in the multivariate context are quite different from those in the univariate tests. This suggests that the findings of a number of previous studies on comparisons of FCEs and LCEs in terms of different parameters based on univariate tests needs a fresh look in view of the interaction between different characteristics.

Third, the analysis of profit margins, provides support for the 'mobility barrier' hypothesis based on strategic differences between groups of firms, in a given industry. The empirical findings support the proposition that FCEs and LCEs constitute different strategic groups and enjoy differential protection from entry barriers. The previous empirical studies identified the strategic groups (leader firms and follower firms) on the basis of their market shares (Newman 1978; Porter 1979). Identification of the strategic groups in this exercise has been on the basis of a more fundamental structural characteristic (i.e., the nationality of ownership connoting several associated differences in the asset bundles, and hence, strategies). Further, the performance of the explanatory variables in terms of the proportion of explained variation differs greatly between restricted and unrestricted profit functions. This suggests that intra-industry heterogeneity is an important determinant of the structure, and needs to be taken care of by future market structure–profitability studies.

Finally, advertising intensity was not found to be related to the profit margins of foreign controlled and local firms. This is of interest because advertising has been posited to be one of the foremost sources of entry barriers in the literature on industrial organization. One of the explanations of this could be the viability of non-advertising–intensive strategies, as indicated by Caves and Pugel (1980). The viability of non-advertising–intensive strategies in India's case, however, could be due to the high degree of seller concentration and insulation of markets from potential competition because of import and industrial licensing.

The estimated empirical relationships and the above findings can also be used as inputs for policy making. For instance, the analysis of the determinants of foreign shares and licensing may help in identifying industries where technology is likely to be available through licensing and where it might have to be secured through direct investment. Hence, the findings may shed some light on policies governing technology imports. The analysis bringing out the inter-group differences in conduct and performance may be useful for policy-makers in assessing the influence of FCEs on different parameters of development, while reformulating the policy towards foreign investments. Similarly, the analysis of profit behaviour brings out the sources of market power of different groups of firms and hence, may be useful for reassessing the policy regarding market competition.

As in the case of any research, this work has limitations arising mainly from data gaps. Given the scope of the database, the study had to exclude the public sector and small private firms. Though the industrial policy defines branches of industry reserved for the public sector and those in which it would play an increasingly important role, in a significant number of industries public sector firms coexist with FCEs and other LCEs. In the analysis of discriminating characteristics of FCEs and LCEs, the size of sample (consisting of 1,334 firms) did not allow us to cover certain other aspects of behaviour which would have required more detailed (and sometimes qualitative) information than is provided in financial statements, such as the cost structures, relative pricing, investment strategy, marketing practices, creation of forward inter-firm linkages, qualifications and experience of employees, working conditions, diversification policy, capacity utilization, and relative dependence on foreign and local sources of technology. Therefore, the study needs to be complemented by detailed industry case studies. Such studies would also be able to control for some more extraneous factors, such as the age of the firm and would be able to capture the dynamic influences of entry of FCEs in an industry. Furthermore, while the study has considered the strategic differences between FCEs and LCEs, in practice, other behavioural differences may exist among firms within these broad strategic groups, such as between sole ventures and joint ventures (among FCEs), and between firms affiliated to large local industrial houses and other independent firms (among LCEs). More detailed firm-level attempts are needed to capture such differences.

that of local firms (Kumar and Siddharthan, 1993). MNE affiliates in India, therefore, appear to be as inward-oriented as local firms.

The industrialization and trade policies pursued over the past four decades within the broad framework of import substituting industrialization made inward-orientation a far more attractive option for MNE affiliates in India as for local firms. The recent changes in strategy to create incentives for export orientation are unlikely to make much difference to the market orientation of existing MNE affiliates in the country. This is because the character of domestic market-oriented and export-oriented FDI is quite different. The export-oriented operations fit somewhere in the vertical chain of production which is globally integrated in the MNE's worldwide operations. Furthermore, for locating export-oriented production a MNE can choose from among many countries. For serving the Indian market, however, their local affiliates would obviously be the natural choice.

In certain countries, such as Mexico, Taiwan, Singapore and Malaysia, MNEs have apparently played an important role in expanding manufactured exports from their host countries. What factors explain the divergent performance of MNEs across countries in terms of export orientation? The success of these countries in expanding manufactured exports through FDI is in fact due to their ability to attract export-oriented FDI. The latter represents investments made by MNEs to relocate their production away from home countries or other industrialized countries in response to rising wage costs. In Malaysia and Indonesia, for instance, about 70 per cent of projects involving FDI have been export-oriented. Thus, only export-oriented FDI and not FDI as such may help in export promotion in host countries.

India has failed to attract export-oriented FDI in any significant measure despite setting up EPZs with the specific objective of attracting MNEs.[2] It may be argued that a liberal and open policy towards FDI will encourage greater inflows of export-oriented FDI too. This need not be the case, however. In a study analyzing the determinants of the inter-country pattern of export-oriented investments, we found an insignificant relationship between FDI and export-oriented investments made by US MNEs across 40 countries (Kumar, 1994). These MNEs were found to be using their hosts more selectively as bases for export-platform investments than for investments in general. Therefore, a greater magnitude of FDI inflow by itself may not help in significantly expanding India's manufactured exports; India should aim to attract a greater volume of export-oriented FDI.

FDIs as Resource Flows

FDI inflows in recent years are increasingly being seen as a means of supplementing foreign aid flows and borrowings for bridging the BOP gap. The policy-makers are hoping to attract about US $3 billion of FDI inflows annually with the liberalized policies.[3] Annual inflows of that magnitude can provide valuable BOP support to the Indian economy. It is argued that these flows are less burdensome for the host economy than commercial borrowings and are self-servicing as the repayments become due only when enterprises start making profits. These premises, however, have a weak basis.

For one, there is a limit to the magnitude of FDI which a low income developing country like India can attract given the stiff competition among developing countries for cornering a greater share of about US $40 billion available for investment in developing countries.[4] Among the factors that determine the distribution of these flows across developing countries various empirical studies (e.g., Root and Ahmed (1979); Scheneider and Frey (1985)) have pinpointed per capita income, growth rate, extent of urbanization, availability of infrastructure, political uncertainty and BOP problems. In light of these findings, low income agrarian economies with BOP problems are likely to attract lower magnitude of FDI than middle income newly industrializing economies (NIEs) with high levels of urbanization. Policy incentives and liberalization have been found to be of limited significance in affecting a country's attractiveness for FDI. During the late 1970s and 1980s a large number of developing countries undertook policy reforms to attract a greater magnitude of FDI. Contractor (1990) in an empirical study of 46 countries did not find liberalization to be an important factor in influencing the pattern of FDI flows.

The foreign investor's response was found to be strongly influenced by the size and growth of the host economy rather than by changes in the government's FDI policies. Another exercise by Wheeler and Mody (1992) covering 42 countries for the period 1982 to 1988 emphasized the importance of the quality of infrastructure, level of industrialization and market size in attracting US FDI. The open market policies or incentives, such as tax breaks were found to be of limited value in determining the investment decisions of US MNEs.

The case of China is often cited as a model of success in attracting large FDI inflows despite its low income characteristics. FDI attracted by China, however, is of a different type, making the comparison with India misleading. For one, bulk of the FDI in China is by non-resident Chinese entrepreneurs settled in Hong Kong and Macao. For them mainland China would be an obvious choice because of cultural and geographical proximity when they decide to relocate labour-intensive production in response to rising wages in their home countries.

During the period 1979 to 1987 for instance, Hong Kong and Macao based enterprises accounted for 79 per cent of total FDI contracts and 67 per cent (US $14 billion) of total committed investment in the country (Chen, 1993). The US, Japan, UK and France have been the main sources of investment from industrialized countries. But over 60 per cent of the total investments pledged from the industrialized countries have been for offshore oil development and not in manufacturing (UNCTC, 1988). It would appear, therefore, that actual FDI attracted by China from the industrialized countries in non-oil manufacturing industries has been relatively small and has been comparable to what India has attracted over the 1980s. Furthermore, while comparing the figures of FDI inflows across countries, one should keep in mind the fact that while India reports only foreign investments involved in approved projects, China and Southeast Asian countries report total costs of FDI projects. This tends to make Indian figures appear much smaller especially because of considerable local participation in equity and local borrowings involved in FDI enterprises in India.[5]

FDIs also have a substantial servicing burden that tends to grow with time. The data provided in RBI company finances studies (RBI, 1992) suggest that 332 FCRCs in the year 1988–89 reported post-tax profits of Rs 777.88 crores on a total paid-up capital of Rs 1622.57 crores which is a 47.94 per cent rate of return. Of the Rs 777.88 crores of post-tax profits, these companies paid out Rs 345.03 crores as dividends to their shareholders (including remittance of Rs 98.62 crores in foreign exchange) and retained Rs 432.86 crores for reinvestments. Thus, the actual rate of dividend remittances even after reinvestment of a part of the profits works out to be 21.26 per cent of the total paid-up capital. As Ashok Desai has noted, 'unlike fixed interest borrowings—the returns on foreign investment would continue to rise as long as companies with foreign capital continue to do well. In the long run, the costs of foreign investment can be extremely high' (1989:81).

It is argued that a servicing burden in the case of FDI arises only when an enterprise makes profits. Therefore, the servicing does not prove burdensome for the host economy. However, one should not overlook the fact that profits earned by FCRCs are in rupees and not in convertible foreign exchange except in select cases of export-oriented enterprises. The 332 FCRCs included in the RBI sample reported a shortfall of Rs 211 crores in the total foreign exchange earnings over their expenditure in foreign exchange. Therefore, dividends remitted abroad in most cases prove to be a burden on the national BOPs even though these are paid out of the profits earned by the enterprises. A World Bank study on India (1989:57) concluded that FDI 'is unlikely to provide a substantial increase in foreign exchange, particularly once repatriations are taken into account.'

The fact that FDI has a substantial servicing burden is clear from Table 8.1 compiled on the basis of the data provided in the *World Debt Tables*. The table shows that the profit remittances by foreign-owned enterprises in developing countries are substantial and have grown over the years. In fact till 1986 FDI inflows in developing countries were not even enough to offset the profit remittances. Hence, the transfer of FDI net of remittances was actually negative. In the subsequent years, net transfers have turned positive because of rapid growth in the magnitude of FDI. Remittances of profits still neutralize over 60 per cent of FDI inflows to developing countries. In the case of moderately indebted low income countries as a group including some of the world's most populous and poorest countries, profits on FDIs exceeded the net FDI inflows throughout the 1984 to 1991 period. Thus, these countries received US $6.4 billion in net FDI flows over this period but were liable to pay $14.5 billion as profit remittances. The relationship between FDI inflows and profit remittances is characterized by a lag due to the gestation period in normal business activity. Therefore, the effect of increased magnitude of FDI inflows over the past few years is yet to get reflected on the profit remittances.

Table 8.1
Flow of FDI to Developing Countries and its Servicing, 1984–1991

(in US$ millions)

Year	*All Developing Countries*			*Moderately Indebted Low Income Countries*		
	Net FDI	*Profits on FDIs*	*FDI inflow net of profit remittances*	*Net FDI Inflow*	*Profits on FDIs*	*FDI inflow net of profit remittanes*
1984	8352	10604	–2252	330	2894	–2494
1986	9576	9956	–380	419	1536	–1117
1987	13468	11139	2329	615	1482	–867
1988	19576	11976	7600	835	1421	–586
1989	23597	13429	10168	950	1888	–938
1990	25240	14130	11110	1355	2187	–832
1991 (Projected)	24706	14996	9709	1400	2444	–1044

Source: Kumar (1992b); on the basis of data provided in the World Bank, *World Debt Tables*, 1991–92.

The justification of FDI as a means of bridging the BOP gap is rather weak. A selective policy targetting export-oriented FDI or high technology FDI may be more favourable for the country's BOP in the end rather than one attempting to maximize the magnitude of FDI irrespective of its composition.

Imperative of Attracting Export-oriented FDI

The foregoing discussion has shown that a greater magnitude

of FDI inflow does not by itself increase the access of the host country to all the associated benefits in the same proportion. Only a selective and target-oriented approach can maximize the benefits of FDI for the host countries. To maximize the benefits from their entry, South Korea, Taiwan and China, among other countries, have been restricting the operations of MNEs to either technology-intensive sectors or export-oriented activities (Westphal et al. 1979; Wade 1990; and Chen 1993 respectively).

In view of the current need to expand exports, India should attach maximum priority to attracting export-oriented FDI. As the determinants of such flows are different from those of domestic market-oriented investment, a more focused approach is needed to attract them. In what follows we discuss the issues involved in attracting export-oriented FDIs and outline relevant policy measures.

Attracting export-oriented FDI is not an easy task given the stiff competition among developing countries. MNEs tend to pick up winners among competing developing countries. In the coming years this competition is likely to intensify further. This is because recession in the industrialized countries tends to reduce demand in these markets. Secondly, with opening up of the East and Central European countries and Vietnam, there is greater competition among countries to attract export-oriented FDI. Finally, increasing protectionism and the formation of trading blocks in the industrialized world discriminates against extra-regional supplies and hence, discourages relocation of production. The Single European Market, for instance, is leading to the substitution of low wage developing countries by Mediterranean countries (especially Turkey, Malta and Cyprus) and East and Central European countries (especially Hungary, Poland and Czechoslovakia) which enjoy preferred access to the European Community (EC) for export-platform production for the EC (Kumar 1992a).

India's main strategic disadvantage is that she does not enjoy special or preferential trading arrangement with either of the triad members (US, EC or Japan). In the past India enjoyed a preferred access to the Soviet Union under a rupee trade arrangement. That had enabled the country to attract a number of MNEs to set up production bases for sourcing the Soviet market. This advantage has also been eroded with the collapse of the Soviet Union.

Most developing countries have set up EPZs to attract export-oriented FDI. The facilities and incentives offered in these zones are comparable and generally include developed infrastructure, tax holidays, free trading environment, and so on. In a recent study Rajiv Kumar (1989:40) reached the conclusion that the package of policy and fiscal incentives offered by Indian zones compared quite favourably with those offered by other Asian zones. While streamlining of procedures and debureaucratization are desirable steps, the scope of further incentives in making India more attractive to export-oriented FDI is rather limited. Empirical studies (cited earlier) have found incentives to be of limited importance determinants. The exports generated by export-oriented FDI are generally of an intra-firm nature. Intra-firm trade is determined more by corporate strategies than by price competitiveness.[6] Hence, currency adjustments may not affect it significantly (Encarnation, 1992).

The magnitude of export-oriented FDI attracted by a country is determined more by structural advantages than by incentives offered. Kumar (1994) in an empirical study analyzing the inter- country pattern of export-oriented FDI made by United States MNEs found the extent of export-oriented investment attracted by a country to be determined by wage levels, industrial capability, infrastructure and the presence of EPZs. The government policy towards FDI (e.g., incentives and performance obligations) or the overall international orientation of the economy did not affect it significantly. Furthermore, the exports generated from such investments depended heavily on the imports from the parent.

India's main strategic advantages over other developing countries are the availability of a large pool of highly skilled and technically qualified manpower at a low cost, a highly diversified and relatively well-developed industrial base which also adds to the availability of experienced engineering and managerial cadres, a large domestic market, and access to primary resources and raw materials, such as iron ore, bauxite and tea. These advantages need to be used more effectively in negotiating with foreign investors.

Large Domestic Market as an Advantage

For MNEs in a number of industries India's large domestic market is an important attraction. This attraction can be used as a bargaining leverage to induce MNEs to set up export-oriented units in the country. This, however, is possible only through a selective policy with respect to entry. The government may identify a number of industries in which the large domestic market may be particularly attractive for MNEs, such as consumer durables and non-durables, and office equipment. Entry into such industries by MNEs may be restricted to proposals having substantial export obligations. China has apparently bargained with the MNEs, allowing entry into her domestic market in exchange for export obligations. According to various surveys 90 per cent of all MNE joint venture contracts in China contained an export provision (Chen, 1993). The export obligations on foreign firms were also imposed for any facilities from official agencies. For instance, their access to foreign loans is contingent upon guarantees by the Bank of China, satisfactory stipulation of production for exports and the provision of advanced technology. Remittances of foreign exchange even after tax have to be approved and are heavily regulated (*ibid.*). Guisinger et al. (1985) have found performance requirements, such as export obligations to be effective in countries with large domestic markets. Kumar and Siddharthan (1993) found some evidence of the effectiveness of export obligations of MNE affiliates in India.

Furthermore, as Wade (1990: 364) points out, export requirements on MNEs would not only generate foreign exchange but would also ensure that companies bring to the country an internationally competitive technology.

Preferential Access to Major Markets

To be a part of a trading block or customs union or a preferential trading arrangement lends a formidable strategic advantage to a country for attracting export-oriented FDI. There is a rush among countries to either join a trading block or secure preferential access to it. A number of Mediterranean, Central and East European countries have secured preferential access to the European Community through various agreements. Many of them, such as Hungary, Czechoslovakia and Poland; and Turkey, Malta and Cyprus are hoping to join the EC eventually as full members. Member countries of the Gulf Cooperation Council (GCC) and the Association of South East Asian Nations (ASEAN) have been having negotiations with the EC for trade concessions (Kumar, 1992a). Seventy African, Caribbean and Pacific (ACP) countries already have preferential access to the EC market under the Lome Convention. Mexico is joining the North American Free Trade Area (NAFTA) with the US and Canada.

It is imperative for India to make a serious attempt to secure preferential access to the European Community. This may enable it to attract Japanese and other East Asian MNEs to set up production bases in the country for sourcing the European market. India should also make an effort to obtain the membership of the ASEAN Free Trade Area, the Pacific Rim Economic Community, and the Asian and Pacific Economic Cooperation which are at various stages of implementation. These memberships could provide India with preferred access to the world's fastest growing markets.

SAARC (the South Asian Association for Regional Cooperation) of which India is a founding member is also forming a SAARC Preferential Trading Area (SAPTA). While SAPTA will not bring India preferential access to any major market, it may help to improve her share in the markets of neighbouring countries.[7]

A Professional Approach to Promotion

In a world of intense competition among countries liberalization of policies and incentives may be important but are not sufficient for attracting export-oriented FDI. Active promotion and courting may often be required. In recognition of this fact the Indian government has set up a Foreign Investment Promotion Board (FIPB) in the Prime Minister's office. The FIPB is composed of top bureaucrats of the economic ministries and is empowered to give one stop approvals. The active promotion of export-oriented investments, however, requires much more than this. For one, promotion of export-oriented FDI is a more specialized task than promotion of FDIs in general. Secondly, it requires professional rather than bureaucratic handling.

The FIPB may be galvanized into the task of promoting export-oriented FDI by creating in it a secretariat consisting of experienced professionals representing the fields of industry, technology and marketing. It should be backed by a strong research department which would continuously monitor, among other things, business strategies and investment plans of the major MNEs, the changing comparative advantage of nations and changes in perceptions and attitudes. The secretariat of FIPB should use various means, such as advertisements in international media, video films and presentations at business conferences and trade fairs to generate wider awareness of the country's strengths, advantages (e.g., availability of various low cost infrastructural facilities, experienced manpower, large domestic market, well developed capital market, availability of minerals and raw materials) and help in creating an awareness about government policies and potential joint venture partners among prospective investors. The FIPB Secretariat may use the overseas offices and infrastructure of other organizations and agencies, such as the Export-Import Bank of India, Indian Investment Centre, and India Trade Promotion Organization, besides coordinating with them in the promotion of export-oriented FDI in India.

Summing Up

MNEs control bulk of world's pool of technology and dominate marketing outlets in all the major markets. FDI is believed to be a major channel to be used by developing countries for tapping these resources for their development. In the current scenario of drying up of soft credit to these countries, FDI is also increasingly seen as a means of bridging the BOP gap.

India's recent liberalization of policies towards FDI in the context of its precarious BOP situation is also based on these hopes. It has been shown, however, that FDI inflow by itself does not bring the associated multiple benefits to the country. FDI dominates advertisement and marketing intensive industries and may not *necessarily* bring in new technologies. Furthermore, technology acquisition through contractual modes as opposed to through FDI may some times be more conducive to building up local design capability in the host country. Similarly, export-oriented FDI alone, and not FDI in general, help host countries in export promotion. FDI as a resource inflows does not appear to be capable of providing significant BOP support to India especially in view of its substantial servicing burden.

In the present scenario, the imperative for India is to focus on attracting a greater magnitude of export-oriented FDI rather than trying to maximize the overall volume of FDI inflows. There is, however, intense competition among developing countries to attract export-oriented FDI. India should use her advantages over her competitors, such as low cost trained manpower and large domestic market more effectively to attract export-oriented FDI. There is also a need to enter into a preferential trading arrangement in at least one of the triad markets. Finally, a professional approach to the promotion of export-oriented FDI is recommended.

Notes

1. See the New Industrial Policy of July 1991.
2. Rajiv Kumar (1989:30) has found the share of foreign investment in Indian EPZs to be low. Only 11 units of the 115 established in the Kandla Free Trade zone and 24 of the 59 operational units in the Santacruz Electronics EPZ had some foreign equity participation including that by NRIs.
3. See the Finance Minister's address at a press conference at the Tokyo Chamber of Commerce and Industry in April 1992 where he expressed 'hope that in the coming two to three years we can get a flow of foreign investment of two billion dollars per annum' (as reported in *The Hindustan Times,* 11 April 1992). Similarly, the Minister of State for Commerce, Mr. P. Chidambaram told a group of potential investors at a meeting in Geneva in May 1992 that India had fixed the target for a total foreign investment of $15 billion by 1997 (see the *Economic Times*, 16 May 1992).
4. Total FDI inflows in developing countries in 1992 were of the order of $40 billion, according to the UNCTAD Programme on Transnational Corporations.
5. In many countries (e.g., Indonesia, Sri Lanka) enterprises with majority foreign ownership are not permitted to borrow in the local capital market.
6. See Siddharthan and Kumar (1990) and Blomstrom (1990) for an analysis of intra-firm trade.
7. See Panchamukhi, Kumar *et.al.* (1990) for the details of the proposed SAPTA.

Appendix

The Database: Sources, Methodology and Definitions

The empirical analyses presented here have drawn data from an exclusive database containing two variable sets assembled for the study. This appendix discusses briefly the sources, coverage, and procedure of compilation of the database. It first examines the nature, scope, and relevance of the official database on FCEs in India. It then deals with the database of the present study and introduces the procedure of its compilation.

Official Database on FCEs

The RBI is the official agency for collecting and publishing data on various aspects of foreign collaboration. The official database in this sector comprises three parallel surveys, described below.

India's International Investment Position

These surveys replaced the RBI's Surveys of Foreign Assets and Liabilities in 1964 and are available up to the financial year ending March 1990. They provide flows in the year as well as stock at the end of the financial year of foreign direct and portfolio investments, with sectoral and source country disaggregation. The surveys present only net liabilities of the country to foreign investors and not the volume of assets under foreign control. They have been useful for analysing the pattern and trends in FDIs in Indian industry, in chapter 1.

Finances of Foreign Branches (FB) and Foreign Controlled Rupee Companies (FCRCs)

In conjunction with their quinquennial series of studies on Finances of Joint Stock Companies, the RBI has also published Consolidated Balance Sheets, and Profit and Loss Accounts of FBs and FCRCs. Though Finances of Public and Private Limited Companies appeared regularly, those of FBs and FCRCs were stopped abruptly after the reference year 1972–73. The RBI has made an attempt to revive this series by publishing finances of 313 FCRCs and FBs (a varying number from 123 in 1975–76 to only eight in 1981). However, this series is inferior to its predecessors in a number of respects. While previous surveys claimed 90 per cent coverage, the present one is not clear about its scope. The industry disaggregation is also reduced, as it now presents data for just seven broad industry categories. The uncertainties of the coverage of the latest survey renders its comparison with previous ones difficult. These have been used by Chandra (1977) and in this study to compute the share of FCEs in the private corporate sector at the overall level.

Foreign Collaborations in Indian Industry

The RBI has conducted four surveys of Indian companies with foreign collaborations providing data on sales, value added, exports, imports, remittances, R&D, etc. These surveys relate to the periods 1960–61 to 1963–64, 1964–65 to 1969–70, 1970–71 to 1972–73, and 1977–78 to 1980–81 respectively. The companies covered have been classified under three groups: majority-owned foreign subsidiaries, minority-owned foreign affiliates, and companies with purely technical collaborations. These surveys together provide a time series for the period from 1960–61 to 1980–81 (barring 1972–73 to 1976–77). Deduction of trends from these is hazardous because neither the number of companies covered nor the industry composition is constant across these surveys. The coverage has varied and was about 25 per cent for the fourth survey. These surveys cannot be used to compare the performance of foreign and local enterprises because not all the minority foreign-owned affiliates (defined with foreign equity proportion between 0 and 50 per cent) have controlling foreign ownership. Second, the industry composition is also not constant across the three categories of collaboration.

For the present study we needed a database which would enable us to quantify shares of FCEs in relatively disaggregated industries and to compare characteristics of FCEs and LCEs in terms of parameters of conduct and performance. It is clear that none of the official databases could fulfil these requirements. Therefore, we had to look for an alternative source of data.

The Database of the Study

For the purpose of the study we needed a database on financial statistics of a large cross-section of companies including both FCEs and LCEs. The RBI conducts quinquennial surveys on Finances of Medium and Large Public Limited Companies. The last series of this survey covered 1,720 companies in the period from 1975–76 to 1980–81. The RBI publishes summary results of the survey in its *Bulletin* for two-digit industry disaggregation.[1] But the summary results do not distinguish between FCEs and LCEs. The basic data file of the survey containing company statistics were acquired but the names of companies had to be held back for reasons of confidentiality.

The Coverage

The database includes each of the non-government, non-financial public limited companies with paid-up capital (PUC) of Rs 10 million or above and a sample from the smaller companies each with PUC of Rs 0.5 million or more. The 1,720 companies selected and included in the database accounted for 86 per cent of PUC of all public limited companies in the private sector in 1979–80.

Industry Classification

Each of the companies included in the data file had been assigned a three-digit code (industry classification) on the basis of the industrial activity that accounts for at least one-half of its turnover. Of the 1,720 companies, 386 had been classified in plantation, mining, and service activities. Since we are confining ourselves to the manufacturing sector, these were excluded from the sample. The remaining 1,334 manufacturing companies had been classified into 62 industry codes.[2] Some regrouping of industry codes was found necessary, which yielded 54 industries, as indicated in Table 2.3.

The major firms in each industry were identified by matching the file data with that reported in the *Bombay Stock Exchange Official Directory*. This helped in checking their given industry codes which needed to be corrected in a few cases. The diversification of firms across different branches posed a problem in some cases. For instance, Hindustan Lever Ltd. (Unilever, UK and the Netherlands), classified in toiletries and chemical products (not elsewhere specified, code 468), on account of the major part of its output being detergents, soaps, and other toilet preparations, is also a market leader in vegetable and hydrogenated oils (code 320). Similarly, Peico Electricals, New Philips India Ltd. (N.V. Philips Holland) is a market leader in electric lamps and fluorescent lights (code 447), but is classified in electrical machinery and appliances (code 448). In such cases the net sales of the companies were split up between the two industry groups they operated in the proportion of sales as reported in their annual reports for the year 1980. This splitting was done only for the purposes of share of FCEs (FS) and the four-firm concentration ratio (CR4). For the rest of the variables, however, the firm was treated to be in the original industry group. DCM and TOMCO were two other companies that were split up.

Identification of FCEs

In the absence of names, the identification of FCEs was done by computing the proportion of foreign-held equity capital and treating a company having at least 25 per cent direct foreign equity as an FCEs, as per our definition (see Introduction). The number of foreign-held shares is revealed in the annual reports only if there are any remittances of dividends to be made in foreign exchange. A few companies that are indirectly foreign controlled (i.e., through controlling interest by other foreign subsidiaries) may not have been classified as FCEs in this procedure as dividends in such cases are remitted in rupees. Furthermore, the dividend may not be remitted in all the years because of profitability fluctuations or management policy. Some companies tend to remit accumulated dividend for a few years at a time. Hence, checking the proportion of foreign equity in any particular year would be inadequate. Therefore, the proportion of foreign-held equity capital was checked for all the six years (i.e., 1975–76 to 1980–81). In addition, our attempt to identify major firms with the help of the *Bombay Stock Exchange Official Directory* enabled us to identify a few FCEs that had been incurring losses and were not likely to be identified as FCEs according to our procedure as there were no remittances of dividends. Of the 1,334 companies included in the sample, 262 were classified as FCEs.

Computation of Variables

The data file after refining the industry classification and identifying the FCEs was used to generate two sets of variables. The first set includes variables that capture industry characteristics, such as share of FCEs in sales (FS), R&D intensity (RDS), advertising intensity (ADS), concentration ratio (CR) and so on, as per the definition given below, for each of the 54 manufacturing industries. The second set includes variables for groups within an industry. In this case the industry was first split up between two 'groups' of firms, namely FCEs and LCEs. The variables were then computed as per the definition for each of the 54 industries, separately for FCEs and LCEs. These variables are suffixed by (i = FCE, LCE) for identification, and are used for analyzing the discriminating characteristics of the two groups of firms.

Variable Set I

An alphabetical list of the 18 variables included in variable set I is as follows (unless otherwise indicated the source of data for all these variables is the date file described above):

ADS: Advertising expenditure as a proportion of net industry sales, averaged over three years: 1978–79 to 1980–81.

AKR: Total capital employed per firm, averaged over three years: 1978–79 to 1980–81.

COR: Total capital employed as a proportion of net industry sales, averaged over three years: 1978–79 to 1980–81.

CR4: Share of top four firms in industry (sample) sales, averaged over three years: 1978–79 to 1980–81.

DCON: A dummy variable, taking a value of one if the industry supplies consumer goods (both durables and non-durables), and zero otherwise.

DCORE: A dummy variable taking a value of one if the industry is included in Appendix I of 'Industrial Policy–Government Decisions 1973', and zero otherwise.

ERP: Effective rates of protection for 1979–80 (Cordon Method). Source: National Council of Applied Economic Research, New Delhi.

FS: Share of FCEs in net industry (sample) sales, averaged over three years: 1978–79 to 1980–81.

GROW: Proportionate change in net industry sales over three years: 1978–79 to 1980–81.

ISP: Potential of import substitution: imports (c.i.f.) to total industry output ratio in 1960–61, computed on the basis of data compiled in Bharat-Ram (1982) from Government of India sources.

LCG: Proportion of licensing of technology and other intangible assets: total royalty, technical, or other professional fees paid abroad as a proportion of net industry sales, averaged over three years: 1978–79 to 1980–81.

PCM: Profit before tax as a proportion of industry sales, averaged over three years: 1978–79 to 1980–81.

PMS: Gross book value of plant and machinery to net sales ratio in 1980–81.

RDS: Reported in-house R&D expenditure as a proportion of net sales, averaged over three years: 1978–79 to 1980–81.

$SKIL_1$: Non-production workers as a proportion of total work force in 1978–79, computed from the *Annual Survey of Industries: Census Sector Summary Results, 1978–79,* Central Statistical Organisation, Govt. of India.

$SKIL_2$: Earnings of high salaried employees (those receiving Rs 3,000 per month or more) as a proportion of the total wages and salaries bill, averaged over three years: 1978–79 to 1980–81.

TECH: In-house R&D expenditure and remittances on account of royalty and technical fees as a proportion of net sales, averaged over three years: 1978–79 to 1980–81.

VAS: Value-added as a proportion of net sales in 1980–81.

In the case of variables ERP, ISP, NPW, for which data was obtained from other sources, the industry classifications were roughly comparable except for a few gaps which were filled by repeating values for the closest industry.

Variable Set II

The variable set II contains 15 variables for two groups of firms (i = FCEs, LCEs) for the same set of 54 industries. All these variables have been computed on the basis of the data file described above. An alphabetical list of the variables included in the variable set follows:

ADS_i: Advertising expenditure of ith group of firms as a proportion of net industry sales in 1980–81.

CUR_i: Ratio of current assets and current liabilities of ith group of firms, in 1980–81.

ERT$_i$: Provision for corporate tax made by ith group of firms as a proportion of their profit before tax in 1980–81.

EXP$_i$: Exports as a proportion of net sales of ith group of firms in 1980–81.

GROW$_i$: Proportionate change in net sales of ith group of firms over 1978–79 to 1980–81.

HIE$_i$: Earnings of high-income employees (those receiving Rs 3,000 per month or above as a proportion of total wages and salaries bill of ith group of firms in 1980–81.

IMP$_i$: Imported raw materials as a proportion of total raw material consumption of ith group of firms, in 1980–81.

INS$_i$: Ratio of inventory to net sales of ith group of firms, in 1980–81.

LEV$_i$: Long-term borrowings of ith group of firms as a proportion of their net worth, in 1980–81.

LKR$_i$: Total wages and salaries bill of ith group of firms as a proportion of their total fixed assets, in 1980–81.

PCM$_i$: Profit before tax of ith group of firms as a proportion of their net worth in 1980–81.

RDS$_i$: Reported in-house R&D expenditure of ith group of firms as a proportion of total sales in 1980–81.

REP$_i$: Retained earnings of ith group of firms as a proportion of total profit after tax in 1980–81.

SIZE$_i$: Average net sales per firm in the ith group in 1980–81.

VAS$_i$: Value added as a proportion of total net sales of the ith group of firms in 1980–81.

Both the variable sets have data for the same 54 industries. For the quantitative analyses presented in chapters 3 to 6, however, five industry groups had to be left out. Levels of competition were not representative in three of them: safety matches and tobacco products (other than cigarettes) due to reservation for the small-scale sector; and iron and steel due to reservation for the pubic sector. The other two industry classes were miscellaneous categories. Hence, data for only 49 observations was used for the empirical analysis.

Notes

1. See *RBI Bulletin* July 1983 for summary results of the year 1980–81.
2. We have included the manufacture of industrial and medical gases, and have excluded printing and publishing from the manufacturing sector for the present sample because of similarity of the former process to that of chemical industries. The latter resembles, in most respects, a service industry.

References

Agarwal, J.P. (1976) 'Factor Proportions in Foreign and Domestic Owned Firms in Indian Manufacturing', *Economic Journal* 86: 529–95.

———(1979) 'Productivity Comparisons in Foreign and Indian Manufacturing', *Weltwirtschaftliches Archiv* 115: 116–27.

Aliber, Robert Z. (1970) 'A Theory of Direct Foreign Investment', in C.P. Kindleberger, *The International Corporation*, Cambridge, Mass. MIT Press.

Amsden, Alice (1989) *Asia's Next Giant: South Korea and Late Industrialization* New York: Oxford University Press.

Arrow, K.J. (1962) 'Economic Welfare and the Allocation of Resources for Invention', in National Bureau of Economic Research (ed.), *The Rate and Direction of Inventive Activity: Economic and Social Factors*, Princeton, NJ: Princeton University Press, pp. 609–25.

Bagchi, Amiya Kumar (1987) *Public Intervention and Industrial Restructuring in China, India and Republic of Korea*, New Delhi: ILO–ARTEP.

Bain, Joe S. (1956) *Barriers to New Competition: Their Character and Consequences in Manufacturing Industries*, Cambridge, Mass: Harvard University Press.

Balasubramanyam, V.N. (1974) *International Transfer of Technology to India*, New York: Praeger.

———(1984) 'Factor Proportions and Productive Efficiency of Foreign Owned firms in the Indonesian Manufacturing Sector, *Bulletin of Indonesian Economic Studies* 70–94.

Baldwin, Robert E. (1979) 'Determinants of Trade and Foreign Investment: Further Evidence', *Review of Economics and Statistics* 61: 40–48.

Bergsten, C. Fred, Thomas Horst, and Theodore Moran (1978) *American Multinationals and American Interests*, Washington DC: Brookings Institution.

Bettelheim, Charles (1968) *India Independent* (English translation), London: MacGibbon.

Bhagwati, J.N. and Padma Desai (1970) *India: Planning for Industrialisation*, London: Oxford University Press.

Bharat-Ram, Vinay (1982) *Towards a Theory of Import Substitution, Exchange Rates and Economic Development*, Delhi: Oxford University Press.

Biersteker, T.J. (1978) *Distortion or Development: Contending Perspectives on the Multinational Corporation*, Cambridge, Mass.: MIT Press.

Billerbeck, K. and Y. Yasugi (1978) *Private Direct Foreign Investment in Developing Countries*, Washington, DC: The World Bank (Staff Working Paper No. 348).

Blomstrom, Magnus (1986) 'Multinationals and Market Structure in Mexico', *World Development* 14: 523–30.

——(1990) *Transnational Corporations and Manufacturing Exports from Developing Countries*, New York: UNCTC.

Bos. H.C., Martin Sanders, and Carlo Secchi (1974) *Private Foreign Investment in Development Countries—A Quantitative Study of the Evaluation of the Macro Economic Effects*, Boston: D. Reidel.

Buckley, Peter J. and Marc Casson (1976) *The Future of the Multinational Enterprise*, London: Macmillan.

Buckley, Peter, J. and H. Davies (1981) 'Foreign Licensing in Overseas Operations: Theory and Evidence from the U.K.', *Research in International Business and Finance* 2: 75–89.

Buckley, Peter J. and Robert D. Pearce (1981) 'Market Servicing by Multinational Manufacturing Firms: Exporting Versus Foreign Production', *Managerial and Decision Economics* 2: 229–46.

Casson, Marc (1979) *Alternatives to the Multinational Enterprise,* London: Macmillan.

Caves, Richard E. (1964) *American Industry: Structure, Conduct, Performance* Englewood Cliffs, NJ: Prentice Hall.

——(1971) 'International Corporations: The Industrial Economics of Foreign Investment', *Economica* 38: 1–27.

——(1974a) 'Causes of Direct Investment: Foreign Firms' Shares in Canadian and United Kingdom Manufacturing Industries', *Review of Economics and Statistics* 56: 279–93.

——(1974b) *International Trade, International Investment, and Imperfect Markets*, Special Papers in International Economics No. 10, Princeton, NJ: International Finance Section, Department of Economics, Princeton University.

——(1982) *Multinational Enterprise and Economic Analysis*, Cambridge: Cambridge University Press.

Caves, Richard E. and M.E. Porter (1977) 'From Entry Barriers to Mobility Barriers: Conjectural Decisions and Contrived Deterrence to New Competition', *Quarterly Journal of Economics* 91: 241–61.

Caves, Richard E. and Thomas A. Pugel (1980) *Intra-industry Differences in Conduct and Performance: Viable Strategies in U.S. Manufacturing Industries*, Monograph Series in Finance and Economics, New York: New York University Graduate School of Business Administration.

Caves, Richard E. *et al.* (1975) 'Scale Economies in Statistical Analyses of Market Power,' *Review of Economics and Statistics* 57: 133–40.

Caves, Richard E. *et al.* (1980) *Competition in the Open Economy: A Model Applied to Canada*, Cambridge, Mass: Harvard University Press.

Chakravarty, Sukhamoy (1984) 'India's Development Strategy for the 1980s'. *Economic and Political Weekly*, 19: May 19–26.

Chandra, N.K. (1977) 'Role of Foreign Capital in India,' *Social Scientist* 57:1.

Chandra, N.K. (1991) 'Growth of Foreign Capital and its Importance in Indian Manufacturing', *Economic and Political Weekly, 26:* Annual Number, March 679–90.

Chaudhuri, Pramit (1978) *The Indian Economy: Poverty and Development*, New Delhi: Vikas Publishing House.

Chaudhuri, Sudip (1979) 'FERA: Appearance and Reality', *Economic and Political Weekly*, 14: April 734–44.

Chee, P.L. (1980) Unpublished MS, cited in Chen (1983).

Chen, Edward K.Y. (1983) *Multinational Corporations, Technology & Employment,* London: Macmillan.

Chen, Jinghan (1993) 'The Environment for Foreign Direct Investment and the Characteristics of Joint Ventures in China', *Development Policy Review* 11: 167–83.

Cheng, Leonard (1984) 'International Trade and Technology: A Brief Survey of The Recent Literature', *Weltwirtshaftliches Archiv* 120: 165–89.

Chung, B.S. and Chung H. Lee (1980) 'The Choice of Production Techniques by Foreign and Local Firms in Korea', *Economic Development and Cultural Change* 29: 135–40.

Coase, R.H. (1937) 'The nature of the firm', *Economica*, new series, 4: 386–405.

Cohen, B. (1975) *Multinational Firms and Asian Exports,* New Haven, Conn: Yale University Press.

Collins, N.R., and L.E. Preston (1970) *Concentration and Price Cost Margins in Manufacturing,* Berkeley: University of California Press.

Comanor, W.S. and T.A. Wilson (1974) *Advertising and Market Power,* Cambridge, Mass: Harvard University Press.

Connor, J.M. (1977) *The Market Power of Multinationals, A Quantitative Analysis of U.S. Corporations in Brazil and Mexico,* New York: Praeger.

Connor, J.M. and W.F. Mueller (1977) *Market Power and Profitability of Multinational Corporations in Brazil and Mexico*, U.S. Senate, Washington, DC, G.P.O.

———(1982) 'Market Structure and Performance of US Multinationals in Brazil and Mexico', *Journal of Development Studies* 18: 329–53.

Contractor, Farok J. (1984) 'Choosing between Direct Investment and Licensing', *Journal of International Business Studies,* Winter: 167–88.

———(1990). *'Do Government Policies Toward Foreign Investment Matter?'* Newark, NJ: Rutgers University (GSM Working Paper No. 90–15).

Cooper, Charles (1985) 'Technical Collaborations between Firms in the Benelux and in India,' *Economic and Political Weekly*, Special Number, November: 2005–22.

Corporate Studies Group (1983) *Functioning of Industrial Licensing System,* New Delhi: Indian Institute of Public Administration.

Courtney, William H. and D.M. Leipziger (1975) 'Multinational Corporations in LDCs: The Choice of Technology,' *Oxford Bulletin of Economics and Statistics* 37: 397–80.

Creamer, Daniel (1976) *Overseas Research & Development by United States Multinationals, 1966–75, Estimates of Expenditure and A Statistical Profile,* New York: Conference Board.

Dasgupta, Ajit and Natteri Siddharthan (1985) 'Industrial Distribution of Indian Exports and Joint Ventures Abroad,' *Development and Change* 16: 159–74.

Davidson, W.H. and Donald G. Mcfetridge (1984) 'International Technology Transfer and the Theory of the Firm,' *Journal of Industrial Economics* 32: 253–64.

———(1985) 'Key Characteristics in the Choice of International Technology Transfer', *Journal of International Business Studies*, Summer: 5–21.

Davies, Howard (1977) 'Technology Transfer through Commercial Transactions', *Journal of Industrial Economics* 36: 161–75.

de la Torre, Jr., J.R. (1974) 'Foreign Investment and Export Dependency,' *Economic Development and Cultural Change* 23: 133–50.

Demsetz. Harold (1975) 'Industry Structure, Market Rivalry and Public Policy,' *Journal of Law and Economics* 16: 1–9.

Desai, Ashok V. (1980) 'The Origin and Direction of Industrial R&D in India', *Research Policy* 9:74–96.

———(1989) 'Foreign Investment—A Time for Rethinking', in *National Conference on Facilitating Environment for Investment and Technology—Conference Papers*, Bombay: Indo-American Chamber of Commerce.

DSIR (1986) *Foreign Collaborations—1985*, New Delhi: Government of India. Department of Scientific and Industrial Research.

Dunning, John H. (ed.), (1974) *Economic Analysis and Multinational Enterprises*, London: George Allen & Unwin.

———(1979) 'Explaining Changing Patterns of International Production: In Defence of the Eclectic Theory,' *Oxford Bulletin of Economics and Statistics* 41: 269–96.

———(1981) *International Production and Multinational Enterprise*, London: Allen & Unwin.

——(1983) 'Market Power of the Firm and International Transfer of Technology', *International Journal of Industrial Organisation* 1: 333–51.

———(1984) 'Non-Equity Forms of Foreign Economic Involvement and the Theory of International Production,' in Richard W. Moxon, *et al.* (eds.), *International Business Strategies in the Asia–Pacific Region: Environmental Changes and Corporate Responses*, Greenwich, Conn: Jai Press.

———(1988) *Explaining International Production*, London: Unwin.

———(1993) *Multinational Enterprises and the Global Economy*, Reading: Addison-Wesley.

Dunning, John H. and Eleanor Morgan (1980) 'Employee Compensation in US Multinationals and Indigenous Firms: An Exploratory Micro Macro Analysis', *British Journal of Industrial Relations* 27: 179–201.

Encarnation, Dennis J. (1989) *Dislodging Multinationals: India's Strategy in Comparative Perspective*, Ithaca and London: Cornell University Press.

———(1992) *Rivals beyond Trade: America versus Japan in Global Competition*, Cornell: Cornell University Press.

Esposito, L. and F. Esposito (1971) 'Foreign Competition and Domestic Industry Profitability', *Review of Economics and Statistics* 53: 343–53.

Evans, P.B. (1977) 'Direct Investment and Industrial Concentration', *Journal of Development Studies* 13: 373–80.

———(1979) *Dependent Development: The Alliance of Multinational, State and Local Capital in Brazil*, Princeton, NJ: Princeton University Press.

Exim Bank (1993) *Foreign Direct Investment in India: India's Policy on FDI—An Overview*, Bombay: Export-Import Bank of India.

Fairchild, Loretta G. (1977) 'Performance and Technology of United States and National Firms in Mexico,' *Journal of Development Studies* 14: 14–34.

Fairchild, Loretta and Kim Sosin (1986) 'Evaluating Differences in Technological Activity between Transnational and Domestic Firms in Latin America', *Journal of Development Studies* 22: 697–708.

Fishwick, Francis (1981) *Multinational Companies and Economic Concentration in Europe*, Paris: IRM.

Forsyth, David J.C. and Robert Solomon (1977) 'Choice of Technology and Nationality of Ownership in Manufacturing in a Developing Country,' *Oxford Economic Papers* 29: 258–82.

Gale, Bradley (1972) 'Market Share and Rate of Return,' *Review of Economics and Statistics* 54: 412–23.

Gershenberg, Irving and T.C.I. Ryan (1978) 'Does Parentage Matter? An Analysis of Transnational and Other Firms: An East African Case,' *Journal of Developing Areas* 13: 3–10.

Giddy, Ian H. and Alan M. Rugman (1979) *A Model of Trade, Foreign Direct Investment and Licensing*, Research Working Paper No. 274A, New York: Columbia University Graduate School of Business.

Gordon, Myron, J. David J. Fowler (1983) 'Performance of the Multinational Drug Industry in Home and Host Countries: A Canadian Case Study,' in C.P. Kindleberger and David B. Audretsch (eds.), *The Multinational Corporations in the 1980s*, Cambridge, Mass: MIT Press, 139–61.

Gorecki, Paul K. (1976) The Determinants of Entry by Domestic and Foreign Enterprises in Canadian Manufacturing Industries: Some Comments and Empirical Results', *Review of Economics & Statistics* 57: 485–88.

——— (1980) 'The Determinants of Foreign and Domestic Enterprise Diversification in Canada: A Note', *Canadian Economic Journal* 3: 329–39.

Goyal, S.K. (1979) 'The Impact of Foreign Subsidiaries on India's Balance of Payments', (mimeo.) New Delhi: Indian Institute of Public Administration.

Gruber, William H., Dileep Mehta and Raymon Vernon (1967) 'The R&D Factor in International Trade and International Investment of US Industries', *Journal of Political Economy* 75: 20–37.

Gruber, William H. and Raymond Vernon (1970) 'The Technology Factor in a World Trade Matrix,' in Raymond Vernon (ed.), *Technology Factor in International Trade*, New York: NBER, pp. 223–72.

Guisinger, Stephen E. *et al.* (1985) *Investment Incentives and Performance Requirements: Patterns of International Trade, Production and Investment,* New York: Praeger.

Gulati, I.S. and Bansal, Swaraj K. (1980) 'Export obligation, technology transfer and foreign collaboration in electronics', *Economic and Political Weekly*, Vol. 25, Special Number, October.

Gupta Vinod K. (1983) 'A simultaneous determination of structure, conduct and performance in Canadian manufacturing', *Oxford Economic Papers* 35: 281–301.

Hathi Committee (1975) *Report of the Committee on Drugs and Pharmaceutical* Industry, New Delhi: Ministry of Petroleum, Chemicals and Fertilizers.

Hay, Donald A. and Morris, Derek J. (1979) *Industrial Economics: Theory and Evidence*, Oxford: Oxford University Press.

Helleiner, G.K. (1973) 'Manufactured Exports from Less Developed Countries and Multinational Firms', *Economic Journal* 55: 21–47.

——(1976) 'Transnational Enterprise, Manufactured Exports and Employment in Less Developed Countries', *Economic and Political Weekly*, Annual Number 247–62.

Hennart, Jean-Francois (1982) *A Theory of Multinational Enterprise*, Ann Arbor: The University of Michigan Press.

Hirsch, Seev (1970) 'Technological Factors in the Composition and Direction of Israel's Industrial Exports', in Raymond Vernon (ed.), *The Technology Factor in International Trade*, New York: NBER, 145–231.

——(1976) 'An International Trade and Investment Theory of the Firm', *Oxford Economic Papers* 28: 258–70.

Hirsch, Seev and Bijaoui, Ilan (1985) 'R&D Intensity and Export Performance: A Micro View', *Weltwirtschaftliches Archiv* 121: 238–51.

Hitris, T. (1978) 'Effective Protection and Economic Performance in UK Manufacturing Industry, 1963 and 1968', *Economic Journal* 88: 107–20.

Horst, Thomas (1972a) 'The Industrial Composition of US Exports and the Subsidiary Sales to the Canadian Market', *American Economic Review* 62: 37–45.

——(1972b) 'Firm and Industry Determinants of the Decision to Invest Abroad: An Empirical Study', *Review of Economics and Statistics* 54: 258–66.

Howe, J.D. and McFetridge, D.G. (1976) 'The Determinants of R&D Expenditures', *Canadian Journal of Economics* 9: 57–71.

Hufbauer G.C. (1966) *Synthetic Materials and the Theory of International Trade*. London: Gerald Duckworth.

Hughes, Kirsty (1986) *Export and Technology*, Cambridge: Cambridge University Press.

Hymer, Stephen H. (1976) *The International Operations of National Firms: A Study of Direct Foreign Investment*, Ph.D. Dissertation (MIT 1960), Cambridge, Mass: MIT Press.

IIPA (1983) 'Political Dimensions of Multinational Corporations', (mimeo.) New Delhi: Indian Institute of Public Administration.

ILO (1976) *Wages and Working Conditions in Multinational Enterprises*, Geneva: International Labour Office.

——(1981) *Employment Effects of Multinational Enterprises in Developing Countries*, Geneva: International Labour Office.

——(1984) *Technology Choice and Employment Generation by Multinational Enterprises in Developing Countries*, Geneva: International Labour Office.

Government of India, Ministry of Industry (1982) *Guidelines for Industries: Part-I*, New Delhi: Indian Investment Centre.

Jackson, Barbara B. (1983) *Multivariate Data Analysis: An Introduction*, Homewood: Irwin.

Jansson, Hans (1982) *Interfirm Linkages in A Developing Economy: The*

Case of Swedish Firms in India, Uppsala: Acta Universitatis Uppaliensis, Studia Oeconomiae Negotiorum 14.

Jenkins, R. (1979) 'The Export Performance of Multinational Corporations in Mexican Industries', *Journal of Development Studies*, 15: 89–107.

Jo, Sung-Hwan (1980) 'Direct Foreign Private Investment', in Chong Kee Park (ed.), *Macroeconomic and Industrial Development in Korea*, Seoul: Korea Development Institute, 129–82.

Johnson, Harry G. (1970) 'The State of Theory in Relation to the Empirical Analysis', in Raymond Vernon (ed.), *Technology Factor in International Trade*, New York: NBER, 9–21.

Johnston, J. (1972) *Econometric Methods* 2nd edn., Tokyo: McGraw Hill.

Katrak, Homi (1980) 'Industry Structure, Foreign Trade and Price-Cost Margins in Indian Manufacturing Industries', *Journal of Development Studies* 17.

———(1983) 'Global Profit Maximisation and Export Performance of Foreign Subsidiaries in India', *Oxford Bulletin of Economics and Statistics* 45: 205–22.

———(1985) 'Imported Technology,' Enterprise Size and R&D in a Newly Industrialising Country: The Indian Experience', *Oxford Bulletin of Economics and Statistics* 47: 213–30.

Kelkar, Vijay (1977) 'Impact of Private Foreign Investments in India, 1964–72: An Economic Analysis', in Charan Wadhwa (ed.), *Some Problems of India's Economic Policy,* New Delhi: Tata McGraw HIll, 729–43.

Khalilzadeh-Shirazi, Javed (1974) 'Market Structure and Price–Cost Margins in United Kingdom Manufacturing Industries', *Review of Economics and Statistics* 56: 67–76.

Kidron, Michael (1965) *Foreign Investments in India,* London: Oxford University Press.

Kindleberger, C.P. (1969) *American Business Abroad: Six Lectures on Direct Investment*, New Haven, Conn: Yale University Press.

Kirim A.S. (1986) 'Transnational Corporations and Local Capital: Comparative Conduct and Performance in the Turkish Pharmaceutical Industry', *World Development* 14: April, 503–22.

Klecka, William R. (1980) *Discriminant Analysis*, Beverly Hills: Sage.

Kojima, Kiyoshi (1978) *Direct Foreign Investment*, London: Croom Helm.

Kumar, Manmohan S. (1984) *Growth, Acquisition and Investment: An Analysis of the Growth of Industrial Firms and their Overseas Activities*, Cambridge: Cambridge University Press.

Kumar, Nagesh (1980) *Evaluation of Direct Foreign Investment in India: A Case Study of Drugs and Pharmaceutical Concerns*, M.Phil. Dissertation, Delhi School of Economics, Delhi University, Delhi.

———(1982) 'Regulating Multinational Monopolies in India', *Economic and Political Weekly* 17: May, 909–18.

———(1984) 'Social Cost-Benefit Analysis of an Export-Oriented Project with Foreign Collaboration in India', *Industry & Development*, No. 10, UNIDO, 9–46.

———(1985) 'Cost of Technology Imports: The Indian Experience', *Economic and Political Weekly* 20: August 31, M103–14.

Kumar, Nagesh (1986) 'Foreign Participation, Market Structure and Employee Compensation in Indian Manufacturing', *Indian Journal of Industrial Relations* 21: 297–309.

———(1987a) 'Foreign Investment and Export Orientation: The Case of India', in Seiji Naya *et al.* (eds.), *Direct Foreign Investment and Export Promotion: Policies and Experiences in Asia*, Kuala Lumpur and Honolulu, Hawaii: SEACEN Research and Training Centre and East West Resource Systems Institute, 357–82.

———(1987b) 'Technology Imports and Local Research & Development in Indian Manufacturing', *The Developing Economies* 25: 220–33.

———(1987c) 'Intangible Assets, Internalisation and Foreign Production: Direct Investments and Licensing in Indian Manufacturing', *Weltwirtschaftliches Archiv* 123: 325–45.

———(1988) 'Foreign Controlled Enterprises in Indian Manufacturing: Overall and Sectoral Shares', *Economic and Political Weekly* 23: November 26, M167–71.

———(1990a) 'Mobility Barriers and Profitability of Multinational and Local Enterprises in Indian Manufacturing', *The Journal of Industrial Economics*, 38: 449–61.

———(1990b) 'Internalisation of Technology Transfers by U.S. Multinationals: A Transactions Cost Perspective', Paper presented at the Annual Meeting of the Academy of International Business, Toronto, October.

———(1991) 'Mode of Rivalry and Comparative Behaviour of Multinational and Local Enterprises: The Case of Indian Manufacturing', *Journal of Development Economics*, 35: 381–92.

———(1992a) '*Single European Market, Multinationals and Industrial Reorganisation: Implications for Developing Countries*, New Delhi: RIS (RIS Occasional Paper No. 37).

———(1992b) 'Resource Flows and Foreign Direct Investments in Developing Countries: Trends and Prospects', *RIS Digest*, 9: 43–56.

———(1994) 'Determinants of Export-Orientation of Foreign Production by U.S. Multinationals: An Inter-Country Analysis', *Journal of International Business Studies* 25(1): 141–56.

Kumar, Nagesh and Kamal M. Chenoy (1983) 'Multinational Corporations in Less Developed Countries: A Case Study of Indian Drugs and Pharmaceutical Industry', *Internationales Asienforum* 14: 175–94.

Kumar, Nagesh and N.S. Siddharthan (1993) *Technology, Firm Size and Export Behaviour in Developing Countries: The Case of Indian Enterprises*, Maastricht: United Nations University—Institute for New Technologies (INTECH Working Paper No. 9): also forthcoming in *Journal of Development Studies*.

Kumar, Nagesh and Mohammed Saqib (1994) *Firm Size, Opportunities for Adaptation and In-house R&D Activity in Developing Countries: The Case of Indian Manufacturing*, Maastricht: United Nations University—Institute for New Technologies (INTECH Working Paper No. 13).

Kumar, Rajiv (1989) *India's Export Processing Zones*, Delhi: Oxford University Press.

Kurien, K. Mathew (1966) *Impact of Foreign Capital on Indian Economy*, New Delhi: PPH.

Lal, Deepak (1975) *Appraising Foreign Investment in Development Countries*, London: Heinemann.

Lall, Sanjaya (1976) 'Financial and Profit Performance of MNCs in Developing Countries: Some Evidence from an Indian and Colombian Sample', *World Development* 4: 713–24.

——(1979) 'Multinationals and Market Structure in an Open Developing Economy: The Case of Malaysia', *Weltwirtschaftliches Archiv* 115: 325–48.

——(1980a) 'Monopolistic Advantages and Foreign Involvement by US Manufacturing Industry', *Oxford Economic Papers* 32: 102–22.

——(1980b) 'Exports of Manufactures by Newly Industrialising Countries: A Survey of Recent Trends', *Economic and Political Weekly,* 15: December 6 and 13, 2051–62, and 2103–12.

——(1981) *The Multinational Corporation,* London: Macmillan.

——(1985) 'Multinationals and Technology Development in Host Countries,' in Lall, Sanjaya, *Multinationals, Technology and Exports*, London: Macmillan, 114–31.

Lall, Sanjaya and Shariff Mohammad (1983a) 'Multinationals in Indian Big Business: Industrial Characteristics of Foreign Investments in a Heavily Regulated Economy', *Journal of Development Economics,* 13: 143–57.

——(1983b) 'Foreign Ownership and Export Performance in the Large Corporate Sector of India', *Journal of Development Studies* 20: 56–67.

Lall, Sanjaya and N.S. Siddharthan (1982) 'The Monopolistic Advantages of Multinationals: Lessons from Foreign Investment in the US', *The Economic Journal* 92: 668–83.

Lall, Sanjaya and P. Streeten (1977) *Foreign Investments, Transnationals and Developing Countries*, London: Macmillan.

Lecraw, Donald (1983) 'Performance of Transnational Corporations in Less Developed Countries', *Journal of International Business Studies* 14 (Spring/Summer): 15–33.

Leipziger, D.M. (1976) 'Production Characteristics in Foreign Enclaves and Domestic Manufacturing: The Case of India', *World Development* 4: 321–25.

Lim, David (1976) 'Capital Utilisation of Local and Foreign Establishments in Malaysian Manufacturing', *Review of Economics and Statistics* 58: 209–17.

——(1977) 'Do Foreign Companies Pay Higher Wages than their Local Counterparts in Malaysian Manufacturing?', *Journal of Development Economics* 7: 55–66.

Maddala, G.S. (1979) *Econometrics*, Tokyo: McGraw Hill.

Magee, Stephen P. (1977) 'Information and Multinational Corporations: An Appropriability Theory of Direct Foreign Investment', in Jagdish Bhagwati (ed.), *The New International Economic Order*, Cambridge, Mass: MIT Press, 317–40.

Mancke, Richard B. (1974) 'Causes of Inter-Firm Profitability Differences: A New Interpretation of the Evidence,' *Quarterly Journal of Economics* 88: 181–93.

Mansfield, Edwin, Teece, D.J., and Romeo, A. (1979) 'Overseas Research and Development by US Based Firms', *Economica* 46: 187–96.

Markensten, Klas (1972) *Foreign Investment and Development: Swedish Companies in India*, Lund: Student Literatur.

Marris, Robin (1964) *The Economic Theory of Managerial Capitalism*, Glances, NY: Free Press.

Marsh, L., R., Newfarmer, and Lino Moreira (1983) *Employment and Technological Choice of Multinational Enterprises in Developing Countries*, Working Paper No. 23, Geneva, International Labour Office.

Martinussen, John (1988) *Transnational Corporations in a Developing Country: The Indian Experience*, New Delhi: Sage.

Mason, R. Hal (1973) 'Some Observations on the Choice of Technology by Multinational Firms in Developing Countries', *Review of Economics and Statistics* 55: 349–55.

McAleese, D. and Donogh McDonald (1978) 'Employment Growth and the Development of Linkages in Foreign-Owned and Domestic Manufacturing Enterprises', *Oxford Bulletin of Economics and Statistics* 40: 321–39.

McManus, J.C. (1972) 'The Theory of the International Firm', in G. Paquet (ed.), *The Multinational Firm and the Nation State,* Don Mills, Ontario: Collier-Macmillan, 66–93.

Meller, Patricio and Alejandra Mizala (1982) 'US Multinationals and Latin American Manufacturing Employment Absorption,' *World Development* 10: 115–26.

Melo, Jaime de and Shujiro Urata (1986) 'The Influence of Increased Foreign Competition on Industrial Concentration and Profitability', *International Journal of Industrial Organisation* 4: 287–304.

Morgenstern, R.D. and R. Muller (1976) 'Multinational Versus Local Corporations in LDCs: An Econometric Analysis of Export Performance in Latin America', *Southern Economic Journal* 42: 399–406.

Morley, S.A. and Smith, G.W. (1977) 'Limited Search and the Technology Choices of Multinational Firms in Brazil', *Quarterly Journal of Economics*, 91: 263–88.

Nayyar, Deepak (1978) 'Transnational Corporations and Manufactured Exports from Poor Countries', *Economic Journal* 88: 59–84.

——(1983) 'International Relocation of Production and Industrialisation in LDCs', *Economic and Political Weekly* 18: PE13–26.

NCAER (1971) *Foreign Technology and investment: A Study of their Role in India's Industrialisation*, New Delhi: National Council of Applied Economic Research.

Newfarmer, R.S. (1980) *Transnational Conglomerates and the Economics of Dependent Development: A Case Study of the International Electrical Oligopoly and Brazil's Electrical Industry*, Greenwich, Conn: Jai Press.

Newfarmer, R.S. and L.C. Marsh (1981) 'Foreign Ownership, Market Structure and Industrial Performance—Brazil's Electrical Industry', *Journal of Development Economics* 8: 47–75.

Newfarmer, R.S. and W.F. Mueller (1975) *Multinational Corporations in Brazil and Mexico: Structural Sources of Economic and Non-Economic Power*, US Senate, Washington, DC: G.P.O.

Newman, Howard H. (1978) 'Strategic Groups and the Structure Performance Relationship', *Review of Economics and Statistics* 60: 417–27.

Oman, Charles (1984) *New Forms of International Investment in Developing Countries,* Paris: OECD Development Centre.

Oster, Sharon (1982) 'Intra-industry Structure and the Ease of Strategic Change', *Review of Economics and Statistics* 64: 376–83.

Owen, Robert F. (1982) 'Inter-Industry Determinants of Foreign Direct Investments: A Canadian Perspective', in Alan M. Rugman (ed.), *New Theories of the Multinational Enterprise*, London: Croom Helm, 238–53.

Pagoulatos, Emolio and R. Sorensen (1976) 'International Trade, International Investment and Industrial Profitability of US Manufacturing', *Southern Economic Journal* 42: 425–34.

Palda, Kristian S. and Pazderka, Bohumir (1982) 'International Comparisons of R&D Effort: The Case of the Canadian Pharmaceutical Industry', Discussion paper IIM/IP 82–6. Berlin: International Institute of Management.

Panchamukhi, V.R. (1977), 'A Quantitative Analysis of Trade Policies in India', in Charan Wadhwa (ed.), *Some Problems of India's Economic Policy,* New Delhi: Tata McGraw Hill, 668–706.

———(1978) *Trade Policies of India: A Quantitative Analysis,* New Delhi: Concept.

———(1987) 'Inflow of Private Capital and Choice of Planning Strategies', in V.R. Panchamukhi, *Planning Development and the World Economic Order*, New Delhi: Radiant.

———(1992) 'South-South Cooperation in South, South East and East Asia: A Perspective', New Delhi: RIS (Discussion Paper).

Panchamukhi, V.R., Nagesh Kumar, *et al.* (1990) *Economic Cooperation in the SAARC Region: Potential, Constraints and Policies*, New Delhi: Interest/RIS.

Parry, Thomas G. (1980) *The Multinational Enterprise: International Investment and Host Country Impacts* Greenwich, Conn: Jai Press.

Pearce, Robert D. and Satwinder Singh (1992 *Globalizing Research and Development*, London: Macmillan.

Phillips, Almarin (1976) 'A Critique of Empirical Studies of Relations between Market Structure and Profitability', *Journal of Industrial Economics* 24: 241–49.

Porter, Michael E. (1979) 'The Structure within Industries and companies' Performance', *Review of Economics and Statistics* 61: 214–27.

Posner, Michael V. (1961) 'International Trade and Technical Change', *Oxford Economic Papers* 13: 11–37.

Possas, M.L. (1979) *Employment Effects of Multinational Enterprises in Brazil*, Working Paper No. 7 (MNE Programme), Geneva: International Labour Office.

Pugel, Thomas A. (1978) *International Market Linkages and US Manufacturing: Prices, Profits and Patterns,* Mass: Ballinger.

———(1980) 'Foreign Trade and US Market Performance', *Journal of Industrial Economics* 29: 119–29.

———(1981) 'The Determinants of Foreign Direct Investment: An Analysis of US Manufacturing Industries', *Managerial and Decision Economics* 2: 220–28.

Pursell, Garry (1981) 'Cost-benefit Evaluation of LDC Industrial Sectors which have Foreign Ownership', Staff Working Paper, Washington DC: The World Bank.

Radhu, Ghulam (1973) 'Transfer of Technological Know-how through MNCs in Pakistan', *Pakistan Development Review* 12: 361–74.

Ragachand, U.K. (1981) 'Characteristics of Research and Development Performing Firms in Canadian Manufacturing', *Research Policy* 11: 193–203.

RBI (1975) 'Finances of Foreign Branches and Foreign Controlled Rupee Companies, 1972–73', *RBI Bulletin*, July.

———(1968, 1974, 1985) *Foreign Collaboration in Indian Industry,* I, II, and IV Survey Reports, Bombay, respectively.

———(1984) 'Finances of Foreign Controlled Rupee Companies and Branches of Foreign Companies, 1975–76 to 1980–81, *RBI Bulletin*, August, 291–360.

———(1985) 'India's International Investment Position, 1979–80', *Reserve Bank of India Bulletin,* April.

———(1991) 'Census of India's Foreign Liabilities and Assets as on March 31, 1987, *Reserve Bank of India Bulletin*, April, 335–417.

———(1992) 'Finances of Foreign Controlled Rupee Companies 1986–87 to 1988–89', *Reserve Bank of India Bulletin*, November: 1817–868.

———(1993) 'India's Foreign Liabilities and Assets as on March 31, 1990, *Reserve Bank of India Bulletin*, August: 1031–1051.

Riedel, J. (1975) 'The Nature and Determinants of Export-oriented Direct Foreign Investment in a Developing Country: A Case Study of Taiwan', *Weltwirtschaftliches Archiv* 111: 505–28.

Reuber, G.L., with H. Crookel, M. Emerson, and G. Gallais-Hamonno, (1973) *Private Foreign Investment in Development*, Oxford: Clarendon Press.

Root, Franklin R. and A. Ahmed (1979) 'Empirical Determinants of Manufacturing Direct Foreign Investment in Developing Countries', *Economic Development and Cultural Change,* 27: 751–67.

Rosenbluth, G. (1970) 'The Relation Between Foreign Control and Concentration in Canadian Industry', *Canadian Journal of Economics* 3: 14–38.

Rugman, Alan M. (1980a) *Multinationals in Canada: Theory, Performance, and Economic Impact,* Boston: Martinus Nijhoff.

———(1980b) 'Internalisation as a General theory of Foreign Direct Investment: A Re-appraisal of the Literature', *Weltwirtschaftliches Archiv* 116: 365–79.

———(1981) *Inside the Multinationals: The Economics of Internal Markets*, London: Croom Helm.

———(ed.), (1982) *New Theories of the Multinational Enterprise*, London: Croom Helm.

Saunders, Ronald S. (1982) 'The Determinants of Inter-industry Variation of Foreign Ownership in Canadian Manufacturing', *Canadian Journal of Economics* 25: 77–84.

Scherer, F.M. (1970) *Industrial Market Structure and Economic Performance*, Chicago: Rand McNally.

Schneider, Friedrish and Frey, Bruno S. (1985) 'Economic and Political Determinants of Foreign Direct Investment', *World Development* 13: 161–75.

Shepherd, William G. (1972) 'The Elements of Market Structure', *Review of Economics and Statistics* 54: 25–37.

Siddharthan, N.S. (1981) *Conglomerates and Multinationals*, New Delhi, Allied.

Siddharthan, N.S. and Ajit K. Dasgupta, (1983) 'Entry Barriers, Exports, and Inter-industry Differences in Profitability', *Developing Economies* 21: 14–23.

Siddharthan, N.S. and Nagesh Kumar (1990) 'The Determinants of Inter-Industry Variation in the Proportion of Intra-Firm Trade: The Behaviour of U.S. Multinationals', *Weltwirtschaftliches Archives*, 126: 581–91.

Siddharthan, N.S. and Sanjaya Lall, (1982) 'The Recent Growth of the Largest U.S. Multinationals', *Oxford Bulletin of Economics and Statistics.*

Siegel, Sidney (1956) *Non-parametric Statistics for the Behavioural Sciences*, New York: McGraw Hill.

Singer. H.W. (1970) 'Dualism Revisited: A New Approach to the Problems of the Dual Society in Developing Countries', *Journal of Development Studies* 7: 60–75.

Singh, A. and G. Whittington (1968) *Growth, Profitability and Valuation,* Department of Applied Economics, Occasional Papers, No. 7, Cambridge: Cambridge University Press.

Solomon, R.F. and D.J.C. Forsyth (1977) 'Substitution of Labour for Capital in the Foreign Sector: Some Further Evidence', *Economic Journal* 59: 283–89.

Solomon, R.F. and K.P.D. Ingham, (1977) 'Discriminating between MNC Subsidiaries and Indigenous Companies: A Comparative Analysis of the British Mechanical Engineering Industry', *Oxford Bulletin of Economics and Statistics* 39: 127–38.

Stewart, Frances (1979) *International Technology Transfer: Issues and Policy Options,* Washington DC: World Bank (Staff Working Paper No. 344).

Stopford, John M. and Dunning, John (1983) *Multinationals: Company Performance and Global Trends*, London: Macmillan.

Strickland, A.D. and L.W. Weiss, (1976) 'Advertising, Concentration and Price-Cost Margins', *Journal of Political Economy* 34: 1109–122.

Subrahmanian, K.K. (1972) *Import of Capital and Technology*, New Delhi: Peoples Publishing House.

Subrahmanian, K.K. and Mohanan P. Pillai (1979) *Multinationals and Indian Export*, New Delhi: Allied.

Swedenborg, B. (1979) *The Multinational Operations of Swedish Firms: An Analysis of Determinants and Effects,* Stockholm: IUI.

Tatsuoka, Maurice M. (1971) *Multivariate Analysis: Techniques for Educational and Psychological Research*, New York: John Wiley.

Teece, David (1981) 'The Market for Know-how and Efficient International Transfer of Technology', *Annals of American Academy of Political and Social Science* 458: 81–96.

———(1983) 'Technological and Organisational Factors in the Theory of the

Multinational Enterprise', in Mark C. Casson (ed.), *The Growth of International Business*, London: Macmillan, 51–62.

Telesio, P. (1979) *Technology Licensing and Multinational Enterprise*, New York: Praeger.

Tyler, W.G. (1978) 'Technioal Efficiency and Ownership Characteristics of Manufacturing Firms in a Developing Country: A Brazilian Case Study', *Weltwirtschaftliches Archiv* 114: 360–79.

UN (1974) *The Acquisition of Technology from Multinational Corporations by Developing Countries*, New York: The United Nations (UN Sales No. E73-II.4.II).

UNCTAD (1983) *Technology Issues in the Capital Goods Sector: A Case Study of Leading Machinery Producers in India*, Geneva: UNCTAD.

UNCTC (1978) *Transnational Corporation in World Development: A Re-examination,* New York: United Nations (E/c.10/38).

———(1981) *Transnational Corporation Linkages in Developing Countries: The Case of Backward Linkages via Subcontracting,* New York: United Nations (E.81. IIA.A.4).

———(1983) *Transnational Corporations in World Development-Third Survey,* New York: UN.

———(1988) *Transnational Corporations in World Development: Trends and Prospects*, New York: UN.

———(1992) *Foreign Direct Investment and Technology Transfer in India,* New York: UN.

UNCTC-ESCAP (1980) *Monitoring and Regulating Transnational Corporations in India*, Working paper No. 12, Joint CTC-ESCAP Unit on Transnational Corporations, Bangkok: UN.

UN ESCAP/UNCTC (1985) *An Evaluation of Export Processing Zones in Selected Asian Countries*, Bangkok: UN (ST/ESCAP/395).

UN-TCMD (1992) *World Investment Report: Transnational Corporations as Engines of Growth*, New York: UN (Transnational Corporations and Management Division).

US Tariff Commission (1973) *Implications of Multinational Firms for World Trade and Investment and* for *US Trade and Labour*, Washington DC: Committee on Finance, US Senate, Government Printing Office.

Vachani, Sushil (1991) *Multinationals in India: Strategic Product Choices*, New Delhi: IBH & Oxford.

Vaitsos, C. (1974) *Inter-country Income Distribution and Transnational Enterprises*, Oxford: Oxford University Press.

Vendrell-Alda, J.L.M. (1978) *Comparing Foreign Subsidiaries and Domestic Firms: A Research Methodology Applied to Efficiency in Argentine Industry*, New York: Garland.

Vernon, Raymond (1966) 'International Investment and International Trade in the Product Cycle', *Quarterly Journal of Economics* 80: 190–207.

———(1974) 'The location of economic activity', in John H. Dunning (ed.), *Economic Analysis and Multinational Enterprise*, London: George Allen & Unwin, 89–114.

———(1977) *Storm over the Multinationals: The Real Issues*, London: Macmillan.

Wade, Robert (1990) *Governing the Market: Economic Theory and the Role* *of Government in East Asian Industrialization*, Princeton NJ: Princeton University Press.

Weiss, John (1980) 'Cost-benefit Analysis of Foreign Industry Investment in Developing Countries', *Industry and Development*, 5: 41–58.

Wells, L.T. (1973) 'Economic Man and Engineering Man: Choice of Technology in a Low Wage Country', *Public Policy* 21: 39–42.

———(1983) *Third World Multinationals: The Rise of Foreign Investment from Developing Countries*, Cambridge, Mass: MIT Press.

Westphal, Larry E., Y.W. Rhee and Garry Pursell (1979) 'Foreign Influences on Korean Industrial Development', *Oxford Bulletin of Economics and Statistics*, 41: 359–88.

Wheeler, D. and A. Mody (1992) 'International Investment, Location Decisions: The Case of U.S. Firms', *Journal of International Economics*, 33: 57–76.

Williamson, Oliver H. (1975) *Markets and Hierarchies: Analysis and Antitrust Implications: A Study in the Economics of Internal Organisation*, New York: Free Press.

———(1981) 'The Modern Corporation, Origins, Evolution, Attributes', *Journal of Economic Literature* 19: 1537–568.

Willmore, L.N. (1976) 'Direct Foreign Investment in Central American Manufacturing', *World Development* 4: 499–518.

———(1986) 'The Comparative Performance of Foreign and Domestic Firms in Brazil', *World Development* 14: 489–502.

Wolf, Martin (1982) *India's Exports*, New York: Oxford University Press (for the International Bank for Reconstruction & Development).

World Bank (1989) *India: Recent Developments and Medium-Term Issues*, Washington DC: The World Bank.

Index